Remembering Beautiful Days in Jerusalem

Shaykh Dr. Mohammad Akram Nadwi

Translation and editing by Dr. Abu Zayd

Al Buruj Press
2023

Published in the UK by Al Buruj Press.

Distributed in the UK by Al Buruj Press.

Al Buruj Press
Masjid Ramadan
9 Shacklewell Lane
London
E8 2DA
Tel: +447947363946
Website: www.alburujpress.com
Email: alburujpress@gmail.com

Second Edition 2023

ISBN: 978-1-915851-02-4

CONTENTS

Publishers Comments ix
Translators Foreward xiii
Introduction by Shaykh Yūsuf Abū Sneina xvii
Hearts Set On The Holy Land 2
Departure, Anticipation 4
In Air At Last 4
Arrival to the Holy Land 5
Jerusalem's Fragrance 6
Eyes on Jerusalem 9
Morning Meal at the Hotel 9
First Group Meeting 10
My Welcome Address: Recognizing Leadership 10
Entry to the Ancient City 13
Bāb al-Ḥiṭṭah ('Forgiveness Gate') 15
Security Search 15
Entering al-Aqṣā Mosque 16
Return from the Mosque 17
Salāḥ al-Dīn Street 19
Ifṭār in the Mosque 19
Dinner at the Hotel 20
Night Prayers at the Mosque 21
Biography of Shaykh Abū Sneina 23
The City Than Never Sleeps 25
Ancient Tombs and Shrines 28
Historical Sites 28
Mount of Olives 29

Shrine of Rābiʿah al-ʿAdawiyah 30
Tomb of Salmān al-Fārisī 31
Tomb of Mūsā 31
The Innovation of Visiting Tombs 33
Hebron 34
Ibrāhīmi Mosque 35
Mausoleums and Tombs 36
A Short Lecture: The Ibrāhīmic Way 38
Bethlehem 40
Church of the Nativity 40
Researching the Birthplace of ʿĪsā 41
The Mosque of ʿUmar 43
Our return to Jerusalem 43
City Walls 46
City Walls 46
King Faisal Gate 47
Temple of Solomon 47
Dome of the Rock 47
Old Mosque 48
The Library 48
The Wailing Wall 49
Moroccan Gate 49
Conversation with some Jews 49
Church of the Holy Sepulchre 50
Mosque of ʿUmar b. al-Khaṭṭāb 50
Ṣalāḥiyyah Khānqah 52
Ṣalāḥī Hospital 52
Back to al-Aqṣā Mosque 53
Bāb al-Raḥmah 53
Zāwiyah of Imam Ghazali 54
The Cemetery of Bāb al-Raḥmah 54

The Cradle of Mary 55
Talk by Shaykh Abū Sneina 55
Teaching in the Holy Land 58
Lesson on Seeking Knowledge 58
Lecture on Death 61
Lesson on the Descent of Jesus 63
Exhausting Walk 64
Great Crowds 66
Pre-Adhān Sermon 66
Friday Sermon 70
Ṣalāḥiyyah Khānqah 74
Place of Khiḍr 74
Lessons in the Land of Ibrāhīm 77
Sa'dī Neighbourhood 77
In the Al-Aqṣā Mosque 78
The Dome of the Lovers of the Prophet 78
Department of Women's Affairs 78
Bāb al-Ghawānimah 78
Bāb al-Nāẓir 78
Bab al-Ḥadīd 79
Bab al-Qaṭṭānīn 79
The Tomb of Muḥammad 'Alī Jawhar 79
Madrasah Asharafiyyah 80
The Dome of Yūsuf 81
Ẓuhr prayer in the Qiblī Mosque 81
Lecture on Patience of the Scholars (Ṣafaḥāt min ṣabr al-'ulamā') 82
Lesson from Iḥyā' 'Ulūm al-Dīn 82
A Lecture after Tarawīḥ Prayers 84
Women's Session 84
Travels from West to East 86
The Tomb of al-Budayrī 86

Al-Burrāq Mosque 87
Museum of Islamic Antiquities 87
Al-Aqṣā Mosque Library 88
Ẓuhr Prayer 89
Lecture from the Patience of the Scholars 89
Lesson from Iḥyā'ʿUlūm al-Dīn 91
Breakfast with the Director of al-Aqṣā Mosque 92
A Short Talk on Supplication 92
Answering Questions 92
Blessed Night 94
Museum of Islamic Antiquities 94
Al-Aqṣā Mosque Library 96
Lessons from the Patience of the Scholars 96
Lesson from Iḥyā' ʿUlūm al-Dīn 99
The Twenty-Seventh Night 100
Meeting with the Women 101
Sermon on the Mount of Olives 103
Zāwiyah Naqshabandī Mosque 103
Bāb Qaṭṭānīn Market 103
Meeting after ʿAṣr 104
ʿIshā' Prayer 104
Sermon on the Mount of Olives 104
Clashes 107
Overlooking the Holy Land 109
Shopping 109
Library 109
Shaykh Yūsuf Uzbekī 110
Answering Questions 110
Lesson on End of Ramadan 110
Mount Mukabbar 111
Lesson on the Mount 111

Expedition 115

Expedition Competition 115

Sighting the Crescent of Shawwāl 116

Women's Meeting 116

Eid on Friday 118

Combining Eid and Friday prayers on the Same Day 118

Eid Prayer 119

Breakfast at the Hotel 120

Friday Prayer 120

Lesson on the Will of Ibrāhīm and Ya'qūb 121

Visit to Jaffa 122

Coastal Restaurant 122

Tel Aviv 123

Our Return to Jerusalem 123

Exploring Outside Jerusalem 125

Al-Eizariya Village 125

Uzair Mosque 126

Al-Quds University 127

Village of Abu Dis 127

Shaykh Ḥusām al-Dīn 127

Excessive Force 128

Lod Gate 129

Indian Hospice 129

Shaykh Abū Sneina 130

Bidding Farewell 132

Shrine of Yūnus 132

Shrine of Prophet Lūṭ 133

Interpretation of the last ten chapters 133

Return Home 134

References 135

Index 138

PUBLISHERS COMMENTS

Jerusalem. What can be said about this holy city? The ancient pebbled streets. The sacred sanctuary where the mighty messengers of God assembled to pray behind the leader of all Prophets, our beloved Muhammad (saw). The very city the great Caliph Umar bin al Khattab (rh) journeyed from Medina by foot/camel to enter in a manner giving meaning to the concept of humility.

Throughout the years, it has been the honour of Al Buruj Press to lead thousands of Muslims on countless trips to the holy land, coined the kingdom of heaven. During our Ramadan 2015 trip, we were blessed to spend the last fourteen nights of the sacred month in the company of Shaykh Mohammad Akram Nadwi. Throughout the journey, the Shaykh diligently recorded notes from all the places he visited to allow those who travel in the future to benefit from his own personal experience, alongside the rich historical information captured along the way. What distinguishes Shaykh Mohammad Akram Nadwi from many others is his sincere desire and ability to capture and present the information in a rigorous and precise manner. A distinguished hadith scholar and author, this approach is evident even in his travelogues.

For those who have visited the holy land, I pray this book brings back beautiful and fond memories. For those planning to visit, God willing, this book will be an invaluable aid to enhance your journey.

There are many who over the years have supported our work in the holy land. To mention a few, Shaykh Omar Kiswani (President of Masjid al Aqsa), Shaykh Yūsuf Abū Sneina (Imam/Khateeb of Masjid al Aqsa) and the amazing group leaders of our al Aqsa trips; Jamal, Abdul Jolil, Uncle Anwar, Farid, Zubair, and Alom. May

Allah reward you all for your love and eagerness towards Masjid al Aqsa. May Allah also reward Dr. Abu Zayd for the rendering, editing and completion of this translation after the initial start by Moulana Huzaifa Nadwi. Ameen.

Zayd ul Islam
Founder, Al Buruj Press

Dedicated to my parents, family and loved ones who support me on a daily basis. You know well who you are. Without your support and love, the trips to al-Aqsa would not be possible.

To the people of Jerusalem, our hearts are with you.

"Glory to Him who made his servant travel by night from the sacred place of worship (Masjid al-Haram) to the furthest place of worship (Masjid al-Aqsa), whose surroundings We have blessed, to show him some of Our signs: He alone is the All Hearing, the All Seeing"

(Surah al-Israa, Verse 1)

TRANSLATOR'S FOREWORD

"Every breath of the believer in this spiritual and blessed atmosphere casts off life's worries and sorrows, as he connects to God, interweaves with His pious worshippers and enjoys the company and presence of the angels."

The blessed city of Jerusalem, in Arabic 'al-Quds,' is one of the precious and dazzling jewels of human civilization. That it occupies center stage in the history and narratives of many different people should come as no surprise. Its place in the Islamic world has been marked by tremendous trauma and pain in the past century, but its rank and position in the faith is no less central.

This is my third labor of love on behalf of my dear and esteemed teacher Shaykh Mohammad Akram Nadwi. In 2015, he embarked on an academic journey to Jerusalem under the auspices of Al-Buruj Press, and ultimately put to eloquent pen his moving experiences and insights in an Arabic travelogue entitled *al-Dhikr al-Jamīl li Ayyām al-Quds wa al-Khalīl*, published in Beirut in 2018. Having previously translated two of his major works as well as numerous articles, Shaykh Akram reached out to me again to translate this particular book. Having missed out on this trip for political reasons (there were security concerns for US travelers in 2015), I gladly obliged.

Shaykh Akram is a seasoned travelogue writer in Arabic. His fluid pen flows with insights, reflections and meticulous observations that are missed by most. There are those that travel with him on international journeys—thankfully, this pleasure has been mine on more than one occasion—and upon return, find his poignant journal documenting an entirely different journey than the one we were on. His heart and mind operate on a different plane of existence than most, and his readers are all the more enriched for that. This is illustrated by the following anecdote in this journal:

> *"I find myself in a delicious dream enticing me with its specters, far removed from the time that I am currently in. People around me ask about me—and I wish that they would stop—but don't they not know that I am in a trance which casts doubts and delusions over my very eyes? Engrossed in the safety of my thoughts, I hear the voice of Zayd informing me that we are in front of . . ."*

His ability to draw the reader into various worlds is remarkable. In the three months I devoted to translating this travelogue, I became immersed in this voyage and truly felt as if I was there. I sensed a great longing for this place that I never knew existed within, and my love for the geography of great prophets increased immensely. He describes the moment they all cast their tired eyes on the city after a lengthy preparatory period:

> *"When we set our eyes on what we were seeing, we found that all the descriptions we had heard from people had missed the mark! A strong fragrance was heavy in the air, spreading its sweet aroma everywhere."*

My vision with these translation projects is to share some of the eloquence and fluidity of the original language into new and self-sufficient English works. A good translation work is one in which the reader is blissfully unaware that it was written in another tongue. For that purpose, literal translation is ill-suited. I have generally tried to reproduce the meaning and intent of Shaykh Akram's words into an English expression that captures their spirit and as much as their letters as is possible. All poetry references have been rendered into independent English verses, utilizing iambic pentameter or the common meter used by poets such as William Shakespeare and Emily Dickinson. I have also taken the liberty of adding chapter headings which were not present in the original Arabic. I have endeavored to provide, as much as possible, all original references for poetry and other quotations, which are listed at the end of the book.

I am indebted to Syed Huzaifah Ali Nadwi, a budding scholar from Shaykh Akram's alma matter who attempted the first draft translation under trying circumstances some years ago. While I have done a fresh translation, I have consulted his work frequently, especially for the more difficult sections. I am also grateful to my diligent proofreader Moiz Mohammed who painstakingly performed the task under the dint of his own deadlines.

I end with a hope and a prayer. My hope is that English readers enjoy the intuitions and lessons from Shaykh Akram Nadwi that this work provides and increase their love for and commitment to Islamic Jerusalem and the land of Palestine. My prayer is that of devoted Muslims and people of conscience around the world: that the misery of the Palestinian people is soon lifted, and that this wonderful and ancient land is freed from occupation and once again opened up to the entire world to enjoy.

Abu Zayd
New Jersey
October 27, 2019 / 28th Ṣafar 1441

INTRODUCTION BY SHAYKH YŪSUF ABŪ SNEINA

Praise belongs to God, and peace and blessings upon the beloved and chosen Prophet.

A group of British Muslims visited us in the last ten days of the month of Ramadan in the year 1436 AH/2015 CE. They came in large numbers, and their ranks included a number of scholars, speakers, and people of knowledge. Among them was an eminent Muslim scholar, a blessing from God for the believers, and a man worthy of mention in the heavens—God willing. He was our beloved brother Dr. Mohammad Akram Nadwi, God preserve him and protect him from every evil. I found him to be a man of real knowledge and practice, one belonging to the ranks of those who are mentioned as models of excellence, precision and deep understanding. He is among those who really live by what they teach. Dr. Nadwi delivered many reminders and lessons in the blessed land, in its holy Mosque and around its sacred rock. His lessons, by the grace of God, affected hearts and minds through their brilliance, insight and eloquence. I grew to love him for his sincerity, strong faith and powerful presence of mind.

We met countless times in the blessed land and holy Mosque. We discussed numerous issues pertaining to beneficial knowledge. I listened to him and he listened to me, in the presence of respected group members of Al-Buruj Press and its leader Ustadh Zayd ul Islam, may God endow him with love for the people of knowledge and righteous scholars. How many wonderful traces and memories in Jerusalem and Palestine were left by our Shaykh Akram, as we sought knowledge in the blessed al-Aqṣā Mosque and in the radiant courtyard of the Dome of the Rock! What blessed times were these and what great company!

By God's grace, Zayd visited us again after five months and brought us a copy of a book written by our shaykh about this joyful journey to the holy land entitled *al-Dhikr al-Jamīl li Ayyām al-Quds wa al-Khalīl.*[1] I read it immediately and found it to be a wonderful and beneficial work, one that absorbs the reader and provides valuable information, all in the most beautiful presentation. I can even say in all honesty that it is far better than what many of our native scholars have written about our land, even though our shaykh is from Britain. It is delivered in a beautiful presentation and style, with extreme precision in its details and authenticity in its information. It includes his meetings with local scholars and contains many wonderful insights and reflections that could only come from a heart that is connected to God and infused with love for His Messenger and for the pious and practicing scholars.

Our esteemed author has spoken about some of the sites he witnessed in al-Aqṣā Mosque and the surrounding regions, providing appropriate comments and insights. He notices details that native residents often miss and shares historical and religious insights that many are unaware of. In truth, I can say that this deserves to be a historical record of Jerusalem and its sites. Were he to expand upon some portions of the book and leave out some which are less relevant, it could be a wonderful and comprehensive presentation of historical sites of the holy land.

In sum, this book is a wonderful model, worthy of praise, of the efforts of the author in writing and documenting his journey. We are immensely indebted to him and extremely grateful for what he has presented to the Islamic nation. I hope that this book can be published in English to benefit an even wider readership.[2]

---

[1] Published by Beirut: Dār al-Bashā'ir al-Islāmiyah. 1439/2018.

[2] These words were written for the Arabic edition, and this work in your hands fulfills this wish.

I ask God to allow people to benefit from this work and reward its author and those involved in its publication. I also thank Zayd for his persistent efforts in visiting al-Aqṣā Mosque. I ask God to place all of this on his scale of deeds for the fateful day when neither wealth nor progeny will avail anyone, and only the pure heart that comes to the presence of God will matter. I thank all brothers and sisters who visited us in blessed Jerusalem and ask God to reunite us in 'gardens and running water, in a seat of truth, in the presence of a Sovereign who determines all things.'

Your brother,

Yūsuf b. ʿAbd al-Wahhāb b. MaḥmūdAbū Sneina al-Maqdisī
Imām of the Blessed al-Aqṣā Mosque
22 Rabīʿ al-Awwal 1439 AH / 11 December 2017

HEARTS SET ON THE HOLY LAND

1

HEARTS SET ON THE HOLY LAND

Sunday 18th Ramadan 1436 AH

Praise be to God and His peace and blessings upon the noblest of Prophets and Messengers—our Prophet Muḥammad, the Seal of all Prophets—and his family, Companions, and those who follow them until the Day of Judgment.

I often get restless from staying in one place and find myself looking forward to exploring God's great earth for recreation and relaxation. I seek to relieve some of the boredom and replace it with enjoyment and joy, in line with the great Arab poet Abū Tamām:

Residing in a place too long
does tire a soul away
So wander far and wide and you'll
refresh your soul anew.

Who does not crave to see at all
the brightness of the day?
But only since the sun does not
forever stay with you[3]

Though I was born and bred in India, it was destined for me to live in the West while yearning for the geographical roots of Islam. My heart is set on Arabia while my origin is Indian; could the agony be any worse? God answered my prayers when he facilitated for me and my family (my wife and daughters Maryam, Fāṭimah and 'Ā'ishah) to spend two weeks in the blessed land of Palestine in

[3] Pg. 26. Ibn 'Asākir. *Tārīkh Madīnat Damishq*. Beirut: Dār al-Fikr.

the holy month of Ramadan in the year 1436/2015. This was the site of the Prophet's Isrā' journey,[4] the land of great prophets and messengers, truthful ones, martyrs, and the righteous, may my life and possessions be sacrificed for it.

Our journey brought together a large number of visitors in an annual program led by our brother and friend Zayd Ul Islam under the Al-Buruj Press organization. Zayd is an intelligent and cultured young person with great managerial skills who has a deep interest in traditional ḥadīth studies and recitals. We were filled with joy and happiness setting off on this blessed journey, overwhelmed with deep emotion difficult to put to the pen.

Become a stranger to your land
Pursue your aspiration
And journey far and wide around,
five things you will attain:

Relief of stress and worrying,
gaining of provision
Knowledge, manners from the pious,
and company of the same.

But do not go at all, some say,
Because of trial and tribulation
The burden of the journey so,
and for its tough terrain.

But over life by far is death
better for a person
Who lives in his own place between
disgrace and stiff defame.[5]

---

[4] The Prophet Muḥammad's miraculous night journey to Jerusalem, referenced in the opening of the 17th sūrah, or chapter, of the Qur'ān.
[5] Pg. 41. *Dīwān al-Imām al-Shāfiʿī*. Maktabah al-Maʿrifah.

Departure, Anticipation

We left Oxford for Gatwick airport, in a London suburb, at 8:15 am. Dr. Shāmikh Sa'īd, an able reciter of the Qur'ān, graciously took us in his car to the airport. We were accompanied by sister Arzoo Aḥmad, who is from Manchester and currently resides in Oxford. At home, I bid farewell to my eldest daughter Husna, her children Abdullah and Aliyah, and her husband Faiz Ullah, may God protect and save them. In the end, I know that my success can only come from God. In Him I place my trust, and to Him I always return.

We arrived at the airport at 9:30 am and found that some members of our group had preceded us there. The total number of people who would be joining us on this auspicious journey were 260, including men and women, most of them from the United Kingdom, and some from the United States, Europe and other countries. In short time, Zayd and the others arrived. They went through the necessary procedures while waiting for the flight departure. In that time, we discussed the details of the journey, our love for the holy land, and our eagerness to spend our time there in worship and God's remembrance. Zayd warned us of some of the difficulties facing Muslims travelers to that region. They are often forced to experience long waiting periods, tough inquiries, and extensive questions at the airport in Tel Aviv, which can take up to six hours or more.

In Air At Last

Scheduled to depart at 12:40 pm, our flight was delayed by more than an hour. We managed to take off at 2:15, and recited the supplication of travel: 'Glory to Him who has brought this [vehicle] under our control, though we were unable to control it [ourselves], and indeed, to Our Lord we will surely return.'[6] After half an hour had elapsed since departure, I went to the back of the plane to pray

[6] Qur'ān 43:13-4.

the Ẓuhr prayer[7] in standing position. While I was praying, there was strong turbulence and the air hostess asked the passengers to take their seats and fasten their seat belts. One of the flight attendants approached me and asked me to go back to my seat. I did not want to go back before missing this chance to complete my prayer, so I completed the ʿAṣr prayer in a seated position before returning to my seat. As there was no place in this small plane for all of us to pray in congregation, I communicated to our group that they should all pray while sitting in their own seats facing the qiblah.[8]

During the course of the journey, Zayd began to introduce the guests to one other. We were all in a state of longing, remembering old times and fondly speaking about Jerusalem. Our yearning made this place which has long been displaced closer to us. Yearning surely makes a distant place closer, and I saw that the place which I have always loved was not so far away now.

We had a light snack in the plane at 8:30 pm and intended to delay the Maghrib prayer to our arrival at the airport. During the flight, my daughter ʿĀ'is5hah felt unwell and began to vomit, prompting the concern of her sister Fāṭimah and their mother, but the flight attendants quickly helped us clean ʿĀ'ishah's seat and her clothes.

Arrival to the Holy Land

The plane landed in Tel Aviv Airport at 9:00 pm. In Hebrew, Tel Aviv means 'hill of spring,' which in Arabic would be written as *tall al-rabīʿ*. The arrival procedures took about two and a half hours, which was far less than we expected. At the airport, we combined Maghrib and ʿIshā' prayers. Being Muslim, we sensed that the leaders of this country were not welcoming towards us but looked

[7] The five obligatory prayers in the Muslim tradition are: Fajr, Ẓuhr, ʿAṣr, Maghrib and ʿIshā'.

[8] The direction of Makkah, which is the direction Muslims face in their prayers.

at us with contempt. Surely, those who expect respect from the wicked are asking for the absurd. On the other hand, the land we were heading towards did recognize us and welcomed us well. It extended to us great honor and touched our weary hearts with its breeze and our tired souls with its warm climate.

This is the land of those noble souls whose love is implanted in our hearts. We cut through vast expanses of time in brief moments that recalled in us those esteemed leaders, warriors, and conquerors from the Companions of Muḥammad, peace be upon him, who were the guardians of God's religion and its borders. We fell in love with them once more, a deep love that could pierce our sides, nay our very hearts!

Jerusalem's Fragrance

We were three buses to Jerusalem, passing through pathways and streets that would have been trodden by prophets, messengers, Companions, scholars and righteous individuals, God be pleased with them all. We inhaled their sweet fragrance and aroma, still ever present around us. This raging wind from the holy land increased our passion even further. We felt as though every part of this holy land had lost a Yūsuf of theirs, while those that remained in the houses was each a Ya'qūb.[9] We finally reached al-Quds around 1:00am. When we set our eyes on what we were seeing, we found that all the descriptions we had heard from people had missed the mark! A strong fragrance was heavy in the air, spreading its sweet aroma everywhere.

Our group was divided into three hotels near Bāb al-Sāhirah (also known as Bāb al-Zahrā or Herod's Gate), one of the gates of Jerusalem's Old City. I stayed with my family in one of these hotels where Zayd and a large number of the group were also staying. The hotel was located in Harūn al-Rashīd Street which is next

[9] From the Qur'ānic story of Yūsuf, full of the pain of a father (Ya'qūb) grieving over his lost child (Yūsuf).

to the horse-riding training center. My room was on the second floor (number 223), a room with a wonderful view overlooking the wall of Jerusalem and the Dome of the Rock. We entered the city comfortable with the words of Imām Shāfiʿī:

Most wise and cultured residents
of any one locale
Find neither rest nor comfort there,
so wander in the wild.

And journey round the world about,
replace the ones you missed
Make sure you leave no stone unturned,
It'll make your life worthwhile.

And water when it stagnates so
Winds up corrupt and putrefied
Pleasant, sweet in stream and flow
And when it stops, it's foul.

Without leaving the den behind,
the lion cannot hunt
Nor can the arrow find at all
a target in the sky.

If were to end and stop at all,
the journey of the sun
Very quickly they would tire so,
all people high and nigh.

And even gold is like the dust,
when settled in the soil
And precious wood in the ground,
is just another pile.

EYES ON JERUSALEM

2

EYES ON JERUSALEM

Monday 19th Ramadan 1436 AH

Morning Meal at the Hotel

We had missed out on dinner and had been subsiding on the dates and water we had consumed on the plane. As a result, we had arrived in Jerusalem in a state of hunger and exhaustion which was more than a little mild. We got to our rooms, unpacked our belongings, and lay down on our beds in order to relieve some exhaustion and calm our nerves and minds. We went down to the hotel restaurant hall at 2:00 am in order to have the suḥūr meal[11] only to find the restaurant doors closed. They would open after 2:30am. When we finally entered the dining hall, we came across a general buffet adorned with Jerusalem-themed decorations. There were various types of Arab food including bread, all types of cheeses, yogurt, eggs, cucumbers, tomatoes, cold drinks, lemon, orange, tea, and sesame sweets. We preferred to eat light snacks briefly and return to our rooms in order to lay down and straighten our backs.

The voice of the adhān[12] of the al-Aqṣā Mosque could be heard in the hotel. Here, at dawn there are two calls to prayer similar to the two Holy Mosques of Makkah and Madīnah: one signaling the night prayer and suḥūr meal, and the second for the Fajr prayer. As soon as we heard the second adhān at 4:00 am, we prayed Fajr prayer in our rooms, as Zayd had advised the group that we would be praying in the al-Aqṣā Mosque only after full instructions were given to us on how to deal with the security personnel, as well

[11] Pre-dawn meal taken prior to fasting from day-break to sunset.
[12] Call to prayer.

as important instructions on entering the mosque precincts and moving between streets and roads.

After Fajr prayer, we slept deeply. I woke up at 10:30 am completely refreshed and feeling no further fatigue or exhaustion. I performed wuḍū,'[13] prayed two rak'ahs[14] and recited from the Qur'ān. My daughters Fāṭimah and 'Ā'ishah came to visit me in my room, and I asked them to take this time to review their Arabic lessons as the date of their exam was soon after we were to return to the UK. I proceeded to write in my diary.

First Group Meeting

At about 12:40 pm, we heard the adhān for Ẓuhr prayer from the al-Aqṣā Mosque and prayed in our rooms again. We gathered in the dining hall for our first group meeting at 3:00 pm. Zayd introduced himself to the guests as the group leader and proceed to inform them of important and required instructions concerning our stay in Jerusalem. He stressed the importance of following the direction of the leader, and not to act impulsively without regard for the group in times of difficulty, for the outcomes of such behavior could lead to banning us from visiting al-Aqṣā permanently.

My Welcome Address: Recognizing Leadership

After these introductory words, I addressed the group beginning by thanking God for having blessed us with this opportunity to visit the holy lands. I asked for His aid in being able to show thanks for His grace, to not waste our time, to do what we can to increase our faith, knowledge and effort; to follow the guidance of the prophets and messengers; and to seek closeness to God and His obedience. I also reminded the group that the full benefit of this visit depended upon observing all the instructions of our group leader Zayd, and that we should always follow our leadership in general. I listed

[13] Ritual ablution with water performed prior to Islamic prayers.
[14] A rak'ah refers to a single unit of prayer.

some verses of the Qur'ān and sayings of the Prophet Muḥammad, peace be upon him, on the obligation and virtue of obeying the leader. I also clarified that if the group leader was to forbid us from praying in the al-Aqṣā Mosque and instructed us to pray in the hotel instead, then obeying his command is better than the one who disobeyed the leader and walked over to the mosque to pray. This would apply even if it were in Makkah itself in front of the absolute holiest mosque. I highlighted that one of the great reasons for the failure of the Muslims today in all aspects of life is our failure to properly organize our religious and worldly affairs, which is linked to our disregard of the duty of obedience and our tendency to break off from the unity of the Muslims.

Then I reminded them about the importance, virtue and blessing of al-Aqṣā Mosque by saying: It has always been God's way in all that He creates and commands that he prefers some things over others. So, for instance, he designated the months of the year and preferred Ramadan over all the other months. He originated days and nights and preferred the ten days of Dhū al-Ḥijjah[15] over all of them. He made Laylat al-Qadr[16] more virtuous than a thousand months. He sent prophets and messengers to humanity and preferred some over others. Similarly, He created the earth and chose some places over others.

I then recited Sūrah al-Tīn and summarized its meanings (which will come later in the section on the Mount of Olives). I directed their attention to the fact that God favored the Arabian Peninsula, the Levant, Egypt, and Iraq over other places. And these are exactly the places where Ibrāhīm lived, emigrated, or walked through. This was all due to God's promise in the Qur'ān:

> *Recall to mind that when his Lord put Ibrāhīm to test in certain things and he fulfilled them all. He said, "I am going to make you the leader of mankind." Ibrāhīm humbly asked, "Does this*

[15] The final month of the Islamic lunar calendar.

[16] The 'Night of Power,' one of the last ten odd nights of the month of Ramadan.

promise also apply to my descendants as well?" He replied, "My promise does not apply to the transgressors."[17]

The leadership continued in those from the offspring of Ibrāhīm who were not wrongdoers and settled in these holy lands. God ordered all prophets and messengers after Ibrāhīm to follow him, even the Master and Seal of all Prophets Muḥammad, peace be upon him:

"Then We revealed to you [O Muḥammad], to follow the religion of Ibrāhīm, inclining toward truth; and he was not of those who associate with God."[18]

This leadership was not the choice of Ibrāhīm but God's gift after He had tested him in certain things which he fulfilled. God does not choose people until after they face many tests and difficulties. Because of that, patience in hardship, forbearance in trivial situations, and the best intentions in thinking and action are the foundations of excellence. God certainly never wastes the reward of the doers of good. There is no value in the lives of those who have lived in luxury and leisure without sacrifice or suffering. People in our time are fond of lives of extravagance and luxury which leads them only to disappointment, failure, and the wasting of the abilities and energy entrusted to them by God.

I also mentioned that Ibrāhīm did not pass any test except that he found the next one to be more challenging than the first. He was always on the road, never settling down and never knowing comfort. He was truly as the Muslim poet Dr. Muḥammad Iqbāl (d. 1938) said: "The home of the Muslim lies beyond the blue sky. You are on a journey in a caravan, followed by stars and planets as dust on the roads." The Muslim is far more valuable than anything in creation. He cannot be bought for any price however high, as the leader of Indian poets Amīr Khusrow (d. 725/1325) said: "You said:

[17] Qur'ān 2:124.
[18] Qur'ān 16:123

You've set your price at the value of both worlds. Raise it higher, for this price is still too low."

It was an address filled with zeal and emotion, which moved some to tears, softened some hearts, elevated spirits and engendered deep contemplation in their minds. I conveyed my advice as best as I could, employing therein the best of my knowledge and thinking. This was in spite of the fact that I was no less in need of guidance than those who were listening, for a person bidding other to do good is no less worthy of taking it up himself. May God bless these words and endow us with speech laden with proper evidences, proximity to the truth and freedom from error. May He bestow us with determination which dominates our base desires, vision that attains guidance and piety, and steadfastness upon the path of righteousness, and, ultimately, our Lord's pleasure.

The meeting ended around 4:00 pm and we finally set out for al-Aqṣā Mosque. Our group was divided into sub-groups and everyone knew their places. My wife and daughters were in the group led by Zayd. He had visited Jerusalem many times and we were delighted to benefit from his knowledge and experience. He would identify streets and places. We were currently on Hārūn al-Rashīd street on the way to the mosque, and he informed us that the street to the right was the well-known Ṣalāh al-Dīn Street. He advised everyone to memorize the name of the street as it was close to our residence in case someone ever lost their way.

Entry to the Ancient City

We entered the ancient city from the north past the boundary walls which were built by the Ottoman Sulṭān Sulaymān the Magnificent. We entered the city finding great comfort in the hopes, aspirations, and traces of the Ottomans which have persisted firmly beyond the passage of heavy time. We journeyed through the narrowest paths and alleyways immersed in antiquity. Shops on both sides sold food, sweets, drinks, clothes, and other commodities of life.

We understood well that Jerusalem has never ceased to be the focus of the world's eyes and the ambition of great kings and conquerors. It has also often been plunged into successive calamities and events, most of them hostile and dim, soiled by the vicissitudes of time.

It is a city full of marvels of civilization, a town that represents the wonders of many lands, and a condensed representation of the entire world. Tamīm Barghūthī (born 1977) said about it:

Jerusalem

Here smoky columns rise about
and marble gives off smoke
And many windows overlook
all church and mosque alike

They grasp the hand of dawn,
to show off color marks
And here aromas do abound,
of India and Babylon

In spice shops of the market places,
great auras all around
I swear, here fragrance speaks with words,
if you would only listen

Hither disputes are pushed aside,
and wonders not denied
Like rich and vivid rags displayed,
from present to the past

Miracles here can be touched,
and marvels with the senses
Shake a gray and aging hand,
or touch a stone or two
And in your palm, you'll find
a verse of poem or two.[19]

[19] Tamīm al-Marghūthī. *Fī al-Quds*. Dār al-Shurūq.

Bāb al-Ḥiṭṭah ('Forgiveness Gate')

I find myself in a delicious dream enticing me with its specters, far removed from the time that I am currently in. People around me ask about me—and I wish that they would stop—but don't they not know that I am in a trance which casts doubts and delusions over my very eyes? Engrossed in the safety of my thoughts, I hear the voice of Zayd informing me that we are in front of Bāb al-Ḥiṭṭah ('Forgiveness Gate'). Al-Aqṣā Mosque is surrounded by an old wall with multiple gates, the most ancient and famous of which is this one, located on the northern wall between the Lions Gates (Bāb al-Asbāṭ) and Bāb Fayṣal. It was built in the era of the Ayyūbid sulṭān and king ʿĪsā Sharaf al-Dīn, nephew of Ṣalāḥ al-Dīn, in the year 617 AH. Perhaps the name of the gate is taken from the verse of the Qur'ān:

> *Then call to mind the time when We said, "Go into the town before you and eat to your hearts' content therein, wherever from you will, but enter the gate bowing down with humility, repeating 'ḥiṭṭatun'"; We will forgive your sins and increase the reward of the righteous.*[20]

Security Search

I was quite surprised to see ill-mannered soldiers armed with weapons outside the gate, and a guard from the blessed al-Aqṣā Mosque run by the Jordanian administration in plain clothes inside the mosque. They were searching everyone entering and leaving in a manner that was extremely rough, harsh, and cruel. We were surprised by such show of force at the very entrance of the blessed holy sanctuary, now providing refuge to pious worshipers and downtrodden frightened individuals. We thought to ourselves that in Europe, India and the rest of the world there exist millions of mosques, churches and temples which are not guarded in this way by any single policeman or soldier. These arrogant people

[20] Qur'ān 2:58.

had gathered at the gates of al-Aqṣā Mosque only to demonstrate their superiority over the Palestinians and as a show of force and contempt towards worshipers and visitors. Our era had become unnecessarily burdened by these despicable individuals. Little do they realize that al-Aqṣā has its own friends and companions, which they do not have. Al-Aqṣā has been ever patient and tolerant of these people, with whom it shares no affinity but only contempt and hatred, for surely the most difficult thing for the noble is to keep company with the wicked.

Entering al-Aqṣā Mosque

We entered the mosque courtyard, a large square containing the Qiblī Mosque (which most laymen mistakenly refer them to as al-Aqṣā Mosque), the Dome of the Rock and other landmarks. It has a total area of more than 144 dunam[21] (150,000 square meters). The Al-Aqṣā Mosque and its landmarks are located on a small plateau called Mount Moriah. The Rock is situated at its highest and most central point. As we walked, beautiful domes rose up to our right and left. Fifteen in number, they are the most prominent feature of the mosque and represent some of the finest specimens of the enduring Islamic artifacts. We saw schools for men and women in the northern and western galleries, some of which extend outside the wall of the mosque.

We walked until we stood right in front of the Dome of the Rock. It dazzled us with its splendor and beauty, and filled our eyes and hearts with great reverence. We wanted to enter it but were stopped as it is used in the holy month of Ramadan as a prayer space for women, while the men pray in the Qiblī Mosque. Those of the women who were with us went inside the Dome of the Rock to pray while we went on towards the Qiblī Mosque.

[21] An Ottoman-era unit of area, roughly equivalent to 1000 square meters. It is still used in Israel today.

We arrived at its prayer space, imagining that this was where so many great prophets and pious people worshipped, bowed and prostrated. These were individuals with traces of the light of guidance over them. They walked with the gait of the humble ones who lower themselves before God with no trace of pride or arrogance. This was our very first prayer in these precincts whose surroundings God had blessed. Our gazes moved about while our fingers pointed everywhere, as coolness set into our eyes. We prayed in congregation with hearts humbled before the majesty and grandeur of our Lord. We reveled in our prostrations—which we considered to be our very salvation and a blessing from God deserving gratitude. We praised God for this grace and favor, before which diminishes all the glitter and glory of this life—its gold, its silver, and its fading objects. What a great blessing it is to be guided to the straight path and to follow in the footsteps of God's pious and truthful worshippers.

Return from the Mosque

We finished praying and returned through the road of the Dome of the Rock. While we were standing at its door, Zayd called Shaykh Yūsuf Abū Sneina, Imām of al-Aqṣā Mosque. I greeted the Shaykh by telephone, and he welcomed our safe arrival and promised to meet us after the 'Ishā' prayer.

Afterwards, we gathered at the Rock jubilant and smiling, our hearts filled with happiness and overwhelmed by a strange feeling that was tempered by a sense of having been chosen and burdened with a great responsibility. We were truly indebted to God for having honored us to breathe in this blessed air which makes even the angels envious. We admitted our weakness in the face of the duty that this had brought to bear on our shoulders—the duty of bearing the trust and delivering the message—imploring our Lord to be pleased with us and allow us to work towards His pleasure.

We listened to the verses of the Holy Qur'ān being read over the microphone by reciters with beautiful voices in the al-Aqṣā Mosque, as is the practice here every day in Ramadan after the 'Aṣr prayer. We exited through Bāb al-Ḥiṭṭah to reach those alleyways that had so quickly become familiar to us, having to traverse them for each and every prayer and visit to the mosque. It was almost as if we had grown up here, as they kindled fond memories of an innocent childhood. It was as if every wall and corner was telling stories from our past, and every stone relating our moments of joy and sorrow, work and play; while being pained by our separation like the departure of a dearly beloved one, or the forced separation of a new bride.

Jerusalem

And to myself said I one day,
perchance this might be good.
But what would you envision in
so brief a journey there?
And would you see those things your mind
can never even imagine?

When on the street appears her house
Not every soul delights
In meeting its beloved one

Nor every separation makes
the lover grieve and weep
And even if they just
were full of such delight

The heart and soul's pure joy
Is no certain prize
But see this ancient place just once
And it will always come to you
Wherever lay your eyes.[22]

[22] Tamīm al-Marghūthī. *Fī al-Quds*. Dār al-Shurūq.

Salāḥ al-Dīn Street

We ascended from the wall of the city onto Ṣalāḥ al-Dīn Street, which represents the very least the city owes to its hero and savior who rescued it from the clutches of barbarians who sowed great corruption, shed blood, defiled honor and violated sanctities. He is the noble knight, brave hero, victorious king, and successful leader Abū al-Muẓaffar Salāḥ al-Dīn Yūsuf b. Ayyūb b. Shādhī (532/1137–589/1193). He ruled over the Fāṭimids in Egypt and liberated Jerusalem and most of Palestine from the Crusaders after defeating them in the Battle of Ḥiṭṭīn in 583/1187. He founded the Ayyūbid state which united Egypt, the Levant, Hijaz, Tihāmah and Yemen under the ʿAbbāssid Caliphate.

Ifṭār in the Mosque

We walked around Ṣalāḥ al-Dīn Street to exchange money and shop for a bit, and returned to the hotel to rest for a little while. We came down at 7:00 pm and set out along with Zayd to pray Maghrib at the Al-Aqṣā Mosque. My family and I were separated again as they joined the crowds of women in the Dome of the Rock.

Zayd and I went to the Qiblī Mosque where we saw tablecloths laid out in the courtyards of the mosque. People sat in various specific spots, each with food and drink laid out according to its sponsors. These included various types of dates, water, yogurt, roasted chicken, bread and rice. I reflected over what I saw in terms of the lack of organization and order in people who were fasting. The manner in which they crowded over the tablecloths was not worthy of the residents of this holy land. Perhaps this had to do with the siege they have had to endure, which inevitably leads to poverty and hardship. We pray to God to increase His abundance to them and all of us through His grace and mercy. The organizers sensed that we were new and humbled us with their welcome and hospitality. When the adhān for Maghrib was sounded, we recited God's name and praised Him while breaking our fasts with dates, water, juice and milk. We compared the atmosphere of Ramadan in our countries with the al-Aqṣā Mosque. Though in our own lands there existed our families, friends and acquaintances, yet here in al-Aqṣā there was an indescribable sense of spirituality, reverence and radiance. This sense is only witnessed elsewhere in the two Holy Mosques of Makkah and Madīnah.

Every breath of the believer in this spiritual and blessed atmosphere casts off some of life's worries and sorrows, as he connects to God, interweaves with His pious worshippers and enjoys the company and presence of the angels.

Dinner at the Hotel

After breaking our fast, we went to the Qiblī Mosque to pray Maghrib in congregation followed by two rakʿahs of sunnah prayer. Then we rushed back to the hotel to eat dinner and rest before returning to the mosque for ʿIshāʾ and Tarawīḥ[23] prayer. We entered the hotel's restaurant and found all kinds food on the serving trays, including meats, vegetables, baked potatoes, rice and breads. We took our seats and soon saw the place crowded with guests who filled their plates with delicious Arab foods and sat at the various tables happy with the joy promised by the Merciful God to the fasting ones. They causally conversed about various things, marveling at the sacredness of the place and the spirituality of the trip, while enjoying the purity of their hearts removed from materialistic and sinful life.

We sat at our tables and exchanged greetings, looking forward to enjoying the delicious food and drink. It was only the first day of our trip, but every time we met one another, it was with great warmth and cordiality, as if we were the closest of family sharing with one another our joys, our sorrows, and our experiences. This was all tempered with a palpable fear of exceeding limits in our speech and conduct. We resolved to force ourselves to eat only the

[23] The nightly congregational prayers in Ramadan during which the entire Qur'ān is customarily recited.

amount needed to give us strength and energy, as the Tarawīḥ prayer lay ahead of us. Overeating and laziness could potentially lead one to miss the congregational and the night prayers. We resisted our impulses to let our hearts become attached to the delicious foods or become prisoners to our desires, and retreated to our rooms to rest and prepare for prayer. I spoke with my wife and daughters about their feelings about this trip, and encouraged them to go to the mosque as much they could. They were well pleased to do so.

Night Prayers at the Mosque

We performed wuḍū' at 9:15 pm and came down to the ground floor where we met Shaykh 'Alī 'Abbāsī, one of the former Imāms of the Dome of the Rock. He welcomed us and was happy for our safe arrival. We accompanied him to the mosque. As we walked, he recounted to us his visits to India as part of the Tablīghī Jamā'ah movement.[24] We exchanged fond memories of our da'wah trips, especially to attend the annual gathering which takes place in Bangladesh, which is considered to be the largest human gathering in the world after the blessed pilgrimage of Ḥajj. God only knows how my heart aches when any comparison is made between Ḥajj and any other gathering. How vast is the expanse between the earth and the heavens? How can a crippled one attain the summits of the strong and sturdy?

The Shaykh talked about the senior scholars of the Tablīghī Jamā'ah movement and their great sincerity and commitment. I recalled how much pain was felt by the founder of the movement, reviver of calling to God, and follower of the Prophetic path, Shaykh Muḥammad Ilyās Kāndehlawī, may God have mercy on him, when Muslims around the world faced weakness in their religion. He was truly as Shaykh Abū al-Ḥasan 'Alī Nadwī wrote:

[24] Religious missionary movement founded in India in 1925 by Mawlānā Muḥammad Ilyās Kāndehlawī (d. 1302/1885) that has a world-wide following in nearly every country of the world today.

> He remembers him as frail, with sharp, penetrating eyes that indicated a deep resolve; he was no orator, indeed he sometimes had a stutter, yet he moved people because "his entire being displayed spirit, vigour, courage, and conviction." He appeared to always be in pain as though "walking on thorny plants," "like someone bitten by a snake." This pain arose from the negligence he saw around him, the inability of human beings to remember how weighty a purpose human life carries, and how grave the consequences are of failing in that purpose. His own realization of that purpose was firm and constant.
>
> His faith in the message brought by the Messengers differed clearly from our faith like the difference between a picture and the reality. His faith in the realities of Islām was more intense and more deep rooted than our faith in the material things and experiences of our life. Anything that was confirmed in the Sharī'ah and established from the Qur'ān and Sunnah was a reality for him in which he had absolutely no doubt whatsoever. It was as though he was seeing the Garden and the Fire with his very eyes.[25]

I reflected over the blessing of his sincerity and commitment in that his work had reached all the way to Palestine, and even beyond that to all remote quarters of the world.

As we continued to walk to the mosque, Shaykh 'Abbāsī asked me about my work to which I gave a brief response. He expressed his great interest in the work *Bustān al-Muḥaddithīn* and his desire to obtain a copy. The book was originally written in Persian by the great Indian ḥadīth scholar 'Abd al-'Azīz al-Dehlawī, son of the renowned star of India Shāh Walīullah. The *Bustān* is about the popular books of ḥadīth and their compilers. I had the privilege of

[25] Pg. 41. Nadwī, Moḥammad Akram. *Shaykh Abū al-Ḥasan 'Alī Nadwī: His Life and Works.*

translating the work into Arabic, which was published by Dār al-Gharb al-Islāmī in Beirut.

We walked among great processions of worshipers heading to the mosque coming out from every nook and cranny. We nearly drowned in this vast sea only to emerge again, all of us spurred on by our yearning for our Lord and great passion settling into our souls—passion which is far greater in those who were visitors from afar.

We reached the Dome of the Rock having missed a few rak'ahs of prayer and joined the prayer outside of Qiblī Mosque. After completing what we had missed, we prayed Tarawīḥ in the main hall of the mosque behind various Imāms who took turns leading the prayer and reciting the Qur'ān with beautiful voices that seized the hearts of people. At the end, the Imām made long supplications in the Qunūt portion[26] of the Witr prayer, repeatedly imploring God to free al-Aqṣā Mosque and the Holy Lands.

After the Tarawīḥ prayers, we made our way to Shaykh Yūsuf Abū Sneina, the Imām of the al-Aqṣā Mosque, who happened to be coming out of the mosque. He welcomed us heartily with a beaming countenance. We were impressed by his complete humility, impeccable manners and lofty character.

Biography of Shaykh Abū Sneina

Shaykh Yūsuf 'Abd al-Wahhāb Maḥmūd Abū Sneina was born on 12th of August 1950 in Jerusalem and received his primary and secondary education in the local schools of Jerusalem. He joined the College of Ḥadīth of the Islamic University of Madīnah in 1977 and studied under many renowned scholars of Madīnah, including the famous ḥadīth scholar Shaykh Ḥammād al-Anṣārī, Dr. Muṣṭafā al-A'ẓamī, the renowned ḥadīth expert Shaykh 'Abd al-Fattāḥ Abū Ghuddah, Dr. Akram Ḍiyā' al-'Umarī, Shaykh

[26] A supplication usually performed in the Witr prayer, which tends to be prolonged in some Muslims communities in Ramadan.

Maḥmūd al-Mīrah, Shaykh Maḥmūd Ṭaḥḥān, Shaykh Muqbil b. Hādī al-Wādi'ī, Shaykh Aḥmad Ṭāhā Rayyān, Shaykh Muḥammad Muntaṣir al-Kattānī, and Shaykh 'Aṭiyah Sālim the student of Shaykh Muḥammad Amīn al-Shanqīṭī. He learned Qur'ān from Shaykh Muḥammad Sālim Muḥaysin, Shaykh 'Abd al-Fattāḥ Qāḍī, Shaykh 'Abd al-Rāfi' Riḍwān, Shaykh Maḥmūd Sībawayh and others. From the great scholars he met were Shaykh Muḥammad Mutawallī Sha'rāwī, Shaykh Sa'īd Ḥawā, Shaykh Muḥammad al-Ghazālī, Shaykh Muḥammad Nāṣir al-Dīn al-Albānī, Shaykh 'Abd al-Qādir 'Īsā, Shaykh 'Abd al-Karīm al-Afghānī and Shaykh Muḥammad al-Qāḍī.

He graduated from the Islamic University with a degree in ḥadīth in 1980. He returned to Jerusalem and was appointed teacher and Imām in the Holy Mosque, where he began to lead prayers. He was appointed principal of Dār al-Ḥadīth in 1985. He was appointed khaṭīb[27] in 1990 and continues to serve this noble function to this day. To date, he has delivered more than three thousand lessons in ḥadīth, tafsīr (Qur'ānic exegesis), jurisprudence, sīrah (Prophetic biography) and other subjects. Currently, he delivers three lessons weekly: an address prior to the Friday prayers, a class on Qur'ānic exegesis on Sundays, and a class on ḥadīth on Thursdays after the Maghrib prayer. Multiple successive generations have benefited from him, to the point that he has tutored many fathers and their sons, grandfathers and their grandchildren. He is blessed with an extremely large number of students, including men and women, and most local Imāms are his associates and students who have been trained by him and have drank from his noble and pure spring.

His written works include a biography of Kamāl b. Abī Sharīf (d. 906 AH), which contains additional biographies of more than one hundred scholars of Jerusalem from the ninth and tenth centuries. He also authored a ten-volume work of Friday sermons entitled *al-Khuṭab al-Maqdisiyah 'alā al-Manābir al-Ṣalāḥiyah*, and a

[27] One who delivers Friday sermons (khuṭbahs).

single-volume 300-page commentary of a single verse: 'Men are the protectors of women.'[28]

We walked with the shaykh towards the parking lot while he spoke at length about the situation of Muslims around the world as well as the harsh conditions experienced by the people of Palestine. I asked him about the scholars of the holy city, especially those who were well-versed in ḥadīth or had an interest in traditional ḥadīth transmission. He responded that there were no great scholars here and that lessons in the mosques always concerned general religious topics. What a pity how the status of Muslims can decline, as Jerusalem once occupied the intellectual leadership of Islam but has since lost that central position. Today, we find remote villages in India that are superior to Jerusalem in knowledge. This is how fortunes are shifted and shares divided by destiny. During our stay, we had numerous meetings and conversations with Shaykh Yūsuf. He is a man of generosity and abundant good, known for his pure character. Gentle and soft, his character does not change with shifting circumstances. His speech is pleasant and sweet which never tires the listener. I have tested and tried many acquaintances, and boredom and fatigue is their most consistent feature.

The City That Never Sleeps

We bid farewell to the shaykh and headed back to our hotels, walking with throngs of people in the streets leaving the mosque. Half the night had already passed, and it was as if Jerusalem never sleeps. On the way, we had ice cream and drinks, and I bought some food. We arrived at our hotel and went to our beds. I was extremely pleased and overjoyed at being in this place. I did not look back for a moment at what I had left behind in terms of the life in England. Here we could achieve perpetual reward and the good pleasure of our Lord. After every night I spend here, I awake with a new resolution. Whoever makes the light of God his guide,

[28] Qur'ān 4:34.

he will find no darkness after that. The most appropriate place for a servant of God is where he can reap the most gains.

ANCIENT TOMBS AND SHRINES

3

ANCIENT TOMBS AND SHRINES

Tuesday 20th Ramadan 1436 AH

We awoke again at 3:00 am, performed ablution and went down to the restaurant to have a light morning meal. We then headed to al-Aqṣā Mosque to perform Fajr prayer and listen to the beautiful loud Qur'ānic recitations. This is the most appropriate time to hear the divine revelation, as God says in His Book: "*And hold fast to the recitation of the Qur'ān at dawn, for the recitation of the Qur'ān at dawn time is ever witnessed.*"[29] We got to the mosque and found its halls empty, unlike the scene previously in the Maghrib and 'Ishā' prayers. I prayed my sunnah close to the position of the Imām. The prayer started at 4:30 am and the Imām recited in the first rak'ah from the last portion of Sūrah al-Kahf and in the second from the last portion of Sūrah Maryam.

Historical Sites

We went back to the hotel and slept until 7:00 am. I took a shower and prayed two rak'ahs of prayer. I then asked my daughters to revise their Arabic lessons while I recited some Qur'ān and wrote in my diary. Today was a day for historical visits. We made our way down at around 8:30 am. Zayd divided the group into two: one would visit al-Aqṣā Mosque and its precincts while the other some other historical sites and cities. My family and I were selected for the latter group. Jerusalem and Palestine continue to be a destination and pilgrimage site since the oldest times, frequented by kings, princes, scholars, and the general public.

[29] Qur'ān 17:78.

We boarded a comfortable bus and were accompanied by Zayd, who was to be our guide for this visit. Before the bus started to move, my daughter ʿĀ'ishah felt unwell so I went to the pharmacy and bought her some medicine. I bought myself some hair oil as I get frequent headaches, especially in Ramadan, and oil relieves the pain. We did not depart until 9:00 am. We left through Hārūn al-Rashīd Street and passed by a small garden on our right, and the wall of the city. The walls of the city were built in antiquity, re-built by Ṣalāḥ al-Dīn (d. 589/1193) and renovated during the reign of the Ottoman Caliph Sulaymān the Magnificent (d. 974/1566) between 1537 and 1541 CE.

Mount of Olives

Our first scheduled visit was to the Mount of Olives, which overlooks Jerusalem from the east. From this place can be seen al-Aqṣā Mosque, the Dome of the Rock, and the neighborhoods, streets and homes of all of Jerusalem. It was named the Mount of Olives due to the large number of olive trees here. You can still find here some trees of massive size and very long age. The place is commonly referred to by people as the Mount of Ṭūr. It is separated from Jerusalem by Kidron Valley, which is said to be the place where ʿĪsā[30] was raised up to the heavens. ʿĪsā would retreat to this place away from the people and preach to them from here. It is written in Luke 21:37: "Each day Jesus was teaching at the temple, and each evening he went out to spend the night on the hill called the Mount of Olives."[31] The New Testament contains some of his sermons on the mountain, and I will mention some of them when we return to the site in one of the coming nights of this blessed month.

In recent times many Jews, especially Americans, are buying plots of land and burying their dead here. This is because they believe that resurrection will take place in this place. We visited

---

[30] Jesus.

[31] New International Version.

a local Jewish cemetery, located in an area which was inhabited by Arabs. A Jewish person owns a piece of land here where he built a house and planted a flag of the newly found state. Yet the Dome of the Rock can be seen from this site like a marvelous and towering sign, high above the rest of the city sites, even though they include other towering buildings, Christian churches and Jewish synagogues.

Shrine of Rābiʿah al-ʿAdawiyah

We then visited the shrine of Rābiʿah al-ʿAdawiyah which is located on the Mount of Olives in what resembles a courtyard and is comprised of many adjacent buildings. The tomb is draped with a garment that bears the writing: "There is no god but God, Muḥammad is the Messenger of God. Surely, the friends of God have nothing to fear, nor shall they grieve."[32] We saw a woman kissing the grave and engaging in other kinds of innovations which are common in places like these. They told us baseless stories of Rābiʿah. And even the historicity of the tomb itself is questionable. The Christians claim that this is a tomb of a saint called Pelagius or Margaret (d. 457 CE), and is considered by the Jews to be the tomb of the prophetess Huldah, one of the women mentioned in the Old Testament.

If indeed the tomb does belong to a Rābiʿah, it is probably the tomb of someone other than Rābiʿah al-ʿAdawiyah. I know of multiple women who had the name, the most famous being the pious and humble worshipper Rabi'a al-ʿAdawiyah of Baṣrah, whose full name was Umm ʿAmr Rābiʿah b. Ismāʿīl. A second was the pious Rābiʿah of Syria, and a third from Baghdad. I believe the one buried here must be the one from Syria. Imām al-Dhahabī (d. 748/1348) writes in his book *Siyar Aʿlām al-Nubalāʾ*: "As for Rābiʿah of Syria, she is less famous than Rābiʿah al-ʿAdawiyah, but their stories are often muddled together."[33] Muwaffaq al-Dīn al-Shāriʿī

[32] Taken from Qur'ān 10:62.

[33] Pg. 243. Volume 8. Dhahabī. *Siyar aʿlām al-nubalāʾ*. Mu'assasat al-Risālah.

(d. 615 AH) states in his book *Murshid al-Zuwwār ilā Qubūr al-Abrār*: "There were many women who have had the name Rābi'ah, but only three of them were famous. They are Rābi'ah al-'Adawiyah, Rābi'ah b. Ismā'īl of Damascus, who happens to share her name as well as her father's name, and Rābi'ah b. Ibrāhīm b. 'Abdullah of Baghdad. The tomb of Rābi'ah al-'Adawiyah is well-known in Baṣrah. Rābi'ah of Damascus died in Jerusalem and was buried on the top of a mountain. She became known by the title al-Qudsiyyah due to her being buried there. However, many common people think that the grave there belongs to Rābi'ah al-'Adawiyah, but this should be clarified. As for Rābi'ah of Baghdad, she was buried in Baghdad."[34]

Tomb of Salmān al-Fārisī

We then walked to the shrine of Salmān al-Fārisī, which is at the southern end of the Rābi'ah al-'Adawiyah road near the tower of the Chapel of the Ascension. The inscription reads: 'Salman is from the Ahl al-Bayt (the household of the Prophet peace be upon him).' The tomb is covered with a shroud, and there is a prayer space in the direction of the tomb. There is no doubt that Salmān is not really buried here, for it is well known that his tomb is in Madā'in.[35]

Tomb of Mūsā

We then boarded a bus and headed to the tomb of Mūsā, peace be upon him. It is located on a mound of dirt in a conical shape, 8 km south of Jericho and 28 km east of Jerusalem. It is an isolated desert region with little shrub or vegetation. It was founded by Ṣalāḥ al-Dīn and expanded by Mamlūk Sulṭān Ẓāhir Baybars (d. 676/1277) in 668/1269. It is a huge two-story building topped by shallow domes in the Mamlūk style, surrounded by a wall with five gates. In its center is an open courtyard composed of three sections,

11th edition.

[34] Pg. 172. al-Sharīʿī. *Murshid al-Zuwwār ilā Qubūr al-Abrār.*

[35] Central Iraq.

surrounded by many rooms, a horse stable, an ancient bakery, and several wells. A cemetery extends around. There is a small mosque with a short minaret towards the north.

The mosque is divided into two sections, separated by a wide wall with an open window. The eastern section is for men, and the western for women, which happens to be smaller in area with a lower floor. The men's mosque has a glazed niche and a green pulpit. Directly to the right of its main entrance is a door leading into a small room topped by a dome and containing in its center a tomb covered with green cloth symbolizing the tomb of Mūsā. To the eastern side, exists a small shrine known as the shrine of Lady 'Ā'ishah. Two kilometers to the west of the shrine of Mūsā is a third shrine called the Shrine of the Shepherd (Maqām al-Rā'ī).[36]

Over the Shrine of Mūsā there appears a ḥadīth from Ṣaḥīḥ Bukhārī where Abū Hurayrah reported:

> The angel of death was sent to Mūsā and when he came to him, Mūsā slapped him severely, harming one of his eyes. The angel went back to his Lord and said, "You sent me to a slave who does not want to die."[37]

Outside the tomb, some of our group members began taking pictures of a small kitten. I said to them jokingly, "This story of the cat is more reliable than the tomb of Mūsā. As far as we know, no tomb site of any prophet has been historically established except for that of the Prophet Muḥammad, peace be upon him. As for all those sites which are claimed to be graves of various prophets throughout the Levant and other places, there is no historical basis for that, and most of these matters are simply fabrications."

---

[36] This is a shrine attributed to a shepherd of Mūsā named Ḥasan Aḥmad Khalīl al-Rā'ī.

[37] Ṣaḥīḥ Bukhārī: Kitāb al-janāiz—Bāb man aḥabba al-dafn fī al-arḍ al-muqaddasah aw naḥwihā.

The Innovation of Visiting Tombs

It pains me greatly to see people praying and supplicating at shrines and tombs, and seeing it as part of religion. These sites have brought about many falsehoods and delusions which have corrupted the faith and convictions of people. As an example, we are currently in the land of the prophets and messengers who called on people to worship God alone shunning all partnerships with Him. But how quickly have people made these prophets a barrier between them and God. They visit their graves and those of other pious people, using them as intermediaries and intercessors to God. They raise their hands in prayer at these sites and kiss their walls for blessings. Ibn Taymiyyah (d. 728/1328) stated:

> None of the Companions made it a purpose of theirs to visit any specific graves: neither the graves of the prophets nor those of anyone else. They neither prayed nor supplicated at these sites nor did they visit them for the purposes of doing so. They never considered it a virtue to supplicate at these sites, nor did they consider supplications at graves to be worthy of being answered.[38]

He also states when talking about the issue of touching and kissing a grave:

> This action is forbidden by the agreement of all Muslims. There is no inanimate object in the world whose kissing is legislated except for the black stone. And this is due to it being established by a report in Bukhārī and Muslim that ʿUmar stated while kissing the stone: "By God I am kissing you, but I know that you are a stone that cannot harm or bring benefit. Had I not seen God's Messenger of God, peace be upon him, kissing you, I would never have kissed you."[39]

---

[38] Pg. 333. Al-Ghaṣn. *Daʿāwā al-Munāwiʾīn li Shaykh al-Islām Ibn Taymiyyah.*
[39] Ibid.

Hebron

As we made our way to our next destination, the famed city of Hebron (Arabic, *Khalīl*), we began reflecting over its inherited past as we set our eyes on its natural sites and the physical traces of the Islamic past. In fact, this entire region is Islamic and Arabic, heir to a glorious past history and advanced civilization. That wonderful past is in fact continuous and uninterrupted to our times. The region remains adorned with a polished, refined and dazzling exterior. It is not like other archeological ruins in remote and desolate places. If you could see its new picture now, reaped as it is by ugly, distorted hands, you would be frightened, and your patience would wear thin. The passing of time over the city has not been kind at all.

When we finally did arrive at the city heights, we began to smell its distinct aroma and sense its Islamic and Arabic character. Located about 26 km south of Jerusalem, Hebron is known for its grapes, camel skins and other products. At its foundation, it was located on a hill in the northwest portion of the current city. It was named after Ibrāhīm, whose title was al-Khalīl, 'God's beloved.' The region has full rights to be attributed to him as he lived a large portion of his life here and walked on its soil.

But the city that is closest to Ibrāhīm is the blessed city of Makkah, which was preferred by God over all other parts of the earth and made a sacred sanctuary in answer to Ibrāhīm's prayer. God has not given this honor to any other city in the world except the city of Madīnah which was also made sacred by virtue of the Prophet, peace be upon him, and followed Makkah in rank, honor, prestige and sanctity. There is no third such city. Jerusalem is simply the city of the third mosque which is a site of pilgrimage in Islam, and not a sacred sanctuary.

Ibrāhīmi Mosque

We entered in the city of Hebron at 1:30 pm heading towards the Ibrāhīmi Mosque. We passed through checkpoints and roadblocks which the Jewish soldiers had put in place with the stated aim of strengthening their own security. But the reality is that God's security can never be granted to those who sow corruption in the earth. Their numbers here are many, and most of the problems and difficulties between the two groups occur due to deliberate intrigues. This makes me jealous of wild animals who are able to coexist without disturbing and oppressing one other, without taking each other's lives unjustly and evicting others from their homes.

The mosque is located in the south of the eastern city over a cavern that is presumed to be the tomb of Ibrāhīm and his family (known as the Cave of the Patriarchs). It is even said that Sulaymān built a wall around this entire cavern and that the Ibrāhīmi Mosque was built over it. A large section of the mosque was closed down after the occurrence of the Hebron massacre of 1994[40] when criminals entered the mosque during Fajr prayers on Friday in the holy month of Ramadan killing twenty-nine worshipers and wounding 150 others. It was then divided into a mosque and synagogue for Jews.

We prayed in the mosque, combining Ẓuhr and ʿAṣr prayers. The mosque is similar to others that were established to accommodate the worship of God and carries the sanctity that characterizes all other houses of God. I was surprised to learn that the general public refer to it as the Ibrāhīmic sanctuary (ḥaram). Is there anyone that can doubt that the sanctuary that Ibrāhīm and his son Ismāʿīl built is '*the one at Bakkah: full of blessing and a center of guidance for the whole world.*'[41]? That is none other than the Kaʿbah which God

[40] Also known as the Cave of the Patriarchs Massacre, it was carried out by American-Israeli extremist Baruch Goldstein on February 24, 1994.
[41] Qur'ān 3:96.

made '*the center and sanctuary for mankind*'[42] and in whose direction commanded people to turn their faces in their worship and sacrifice. That alone is the place about which God has said: '*Pilgrimage to the House is a duty owed to God by all who can make their way to it.*'[43]

Mausoleums and Tombs

We remained in the mosque until 3:15 pm, during which time we visited the shrines which house the tombs of Ibrāhīm, Isḥāq and Ya'qūb, along with their spouses Sarah, Rebecca, and Leah. There is no historical document confirming that this is in fact their burial place. It is likely that Ya'qūb was buried in Egypt where he died along with his family and children. In the Qur'ān, God mentions the commandment of Ya'qūb to his sons when he was approaching his death and there is no proof that he migrated with his sons prior to his death to the Levant. It is also difficult to imagine that his body would have been later taken to the Levant as prophets are generally buried where they die.

Historians generally agree that Ibrāhīm was buried in this general region without being certain of the exact location. Ibn Kathīr said:

> His (Ibrāhīm's) grave, that of his son Isḥāq and grandson Ya'qūb are located in the square built by Sulaymān in the land of Hebron which is known as Khalīl today. This report is transmitted en masse generation after generation, from the time of the Israelites until out times: that his grave is in the square. As for the exact place for each prophet, then there is no sound report concerning that.[44]

However, Ibn Kathīr is not correct in his assertion that the report concerning Ya'qūb's grave being there is mass-transmitted. Ibn Taymiyyah states:

---

[42] Qur'ān 2:125.
[43] Qur'ān 3:97.
[44] Pg. 212. Ibn Kathīr, *al-Bidāyah wa al-Nihāyah.*

Taking gravesites as mosques or building mosques over graves has been categorically forbidden. None of that existed in the time of the Companions or Followers. There was no known mosque over a gravesite. Even Ibrāhīm was buried in a cave which was closed to anyone entering. No Companions were known to have ever visited there or any other gravesite for that matter. Bukhārī and Muslim both relate from Abū Hurayrah and Abū Saʿīd that the Prophet, peace be upon him, said: "Do not undertake a journey to visit any mosque except for three: the Mosque of al-Ḥaram (Makkah), the Mosque of al-Aqṣā, and this Mosque of mine."[45] So they would visit al-Aqṣā Mosque, and return without visiting the Cave of Ibrāhīm or other sites.

Moreover, the Cave was always closed until the Christian rule over the Levant in the end of the fourth century, during which time they opened it up and made a church at the site. When the Muslims ruled over the area, some of them used the site as a mosque, although scholars deemed that disliked. As for what some of them narrated concerning the ḥadīth of Isrāʾ in which he reportedly stopped and prayed in this site, it is an absolute fabrication. The Prophet, peace be upon him, on that night only prayed in al-Aqṣā, for that is the only place he stopped at, as established by a report from Ṣaḥīḥ Bukhārī.

Because of this, large numbers of Companions began to visit, including ʿUmar when he conquered Jerusalem. After he conquered the Levant, ʿUmar came here again to conclude a mutual agreement with the Christians and institute the jizyah protection tax with its well-known conditions. During a third visit, he arrived to Sargh with a large group of the senior Companions. In all of these

[45] Ṣaḥīḥ Bukhārī: Kitāb Faḍl al-Ṣalāh fī Masjid Makkah wa al-Madīnah—Bāb Faḍl al-Ṣalāh fī Masjid Makkah wa al-Madīnah.

visits, none of the Companions were known to visit the Cave or any other sites related to the prophets, anywhere in the Levant, Jerusalem, Damascus or anywhere else.[46]

In all of these instances, not a single Companion visited the Cave of Ibrāhīm, which only had a small building over the cave at the time which remained closed without any door, much like the grave of the Prophet, peace be upon him. It remained so in the Umayyad and ʿAbbāsid eras until a Christian king in the fifth century built the current structure, constructed a church therein and opened a door. That is why you find a door that is excavated and not constructed. When the Muslims regained the region, some people converted it to a mosque.[47]

No Companion or Follower ever came to the grave of Ibrāhīm to pray, to make supplications, or even just to visit.[48]

A Short Lecture: The Ibrāhīmic Way

I delivered a lecture in the mosque in which I affirmed that we do not know the exact location of the graves of any prophet except for the location of the grave of the Prophet Muḥammad, peace be upon him, and that this does not harm the prophets in the least. The prophets were sent to connect people with their Lord. What is important to us are their teachings. In the case of Ibrāhīm, God preserved the very sum and substance of Ibrāhīm's way and manner throughout the Qurʾān.

[46] Pg. 249-50. Volume 17. Ibn Taymiyyah. *Majmūʿ al-Fatāwā*. Dār al-Wafāʾ.
[47] Pg. 291-2. Volume 4. Ibn Taymiyyah. *Al-Tafsīr al-Kabīr*.
[48] Ibn Taymiyyah, *Majmūʿ al-Fatāwā*. 17/464-465.

I explained the meaning of the ḥanīfiyyah path[49] which Ibrāhīm adopted along with the great eloquence of his words: "*Behold, I have turned my face in exclusive devotion to the One Who originated the heavens and the earth, and I am certainly not one of those who associate others with Allah in His divinity.*"[50] This means that we should worship none but God, supplicate to none but God, and not associate with Him in any way, shape or form. It also means to halt at the limits set by God and His Messenger, which is what it means to be guided. It means to avoid all innovations, which inevitably lead to misguidance. The insightful believer must be in control over his desires. He must never accept any statement without verifying it first, and not persist in falsehood when it is made apparent.

The audience then asked a series of questions, which included questions such as 'Which Prophet was greater, the Prophet Muḥammad, peace be upon him, or Ibrāhīm?'; questions on the history of Hebron, Jerusalem, the descent of 'Īsā, and others. I responded to all of those appropriately. There was also a question about the supposed migration of Ismā'īl and his children to the Levant, to which I responded that he had not migrated but come here only for the purposes of trade.

Finally, I reminded all that God had intended to strengthen our bond with Ibrāhīm, because he was the leader of all men in the notion of ḥanīfiyyah, pure monotheism (tawḥīd) and total submission to God. He was our role-model in faith. I ask God to teach us that which is beneficial and make us pure monotheists avoiding every vestige of shirk.

---

[49] According to Dr. Akram, the term *ḥanīfiyyah* refers to the most important element of the Ibrāhīmic way (millat Ibrāhīm) that is encapsulated in the Qur'ān: to cut oneself off from everything finite in the world in favor of the infinite and everlasting Lord of all the worlds.
[50] Qur'ān 6:79.

Bethlehem

We left Hebron at 3:30 pm only to be confronted by another checkpoint manned by those who appeared to hate us and care little about God's sanctity. Those who possess two colors can never be consistent towards creation, but are instead often treacherous and sinful towards many of them. We arrived in Bethlehem at 4:30 pm. It is 10 km south of Jerusalem. Its history extends beyond the Christian era. First inhabited by the Canaanites, it was named after their god of fertility Lehem. It became an important historical city because of the popular belief that 'Īsā was born there. It came under the Muslim fold during the reign of 'Umar when the Levant was opened. It came again under Christian rule during the Crusades, only to be liberated by the pious ruler Ṣalāh al-Dīn after the battle of Ḥiṭṭīn. Today, it remains under the jurisdiction of the Palestinian authority.

Church of the Nativity

We wandered inside Bethlehem heading towards the Church of the Nativity and the Mosque of 'Umar. We began exploring the church, which happens to be one of the oldest and most venerated churches in the world and a frequent pilgrimage site. Named in reference to the cradle of 'Īsā, it was built by Emperor Constantine in the year 335 CE with a structure resembling Roman temples. It contains the cave where 'Īsā was supposedly born, which is now adorned with white marble floors which also extend to the church courtyards. It is surrounded by a large church where rituals are held by several monasteries from various Christian sects.

We were repulsed by the many pictures and statues of 'Īsā and Maryam, which made the quarters resemble pagan temples. How could this be a destination for those who ascribe themselves to great prophets and messengers? God is remembered here very little, and they are far from real guidance, with little concern for the pure and straight path, true faith in God or true submission to the Lord of the worlds. They are now a people unaware of worship, ritual and humility; oblivious to the Day of Judgement where all people will be held to account and divided into two groups: one for Paradise and one for the Fire. How difficult it now appears to reverse their transgression or restore their guidance, for the Qur'ān came down and did not help them come back to guidance. It is like the bright day which increases the vision of those who can see and increases the blindness of creatures like the bats. The wise one is never content nor self-deluded with a situation that only leads to corruption, and will never bow before any creation whose end is decline and death. May God guide us to the straight path and help us avoid shirk and its practitioners.

Researching the Birthplace of 'Īsā

I am skeptical about the birth of 'Īsā in this place and believe that some Christians may have fabricated the story of the birth here in order to create a center for themselves, not unlike their mistake concerning the date of 'Īsā's birth, or their greater lie, slander and falsehood about Jesus being the son of God. In this journey, I will be passing through many places which are attributed to 'Īsā. Christians have muddled up the story so I would like to firstly convey what the Qur'ān says about his birth:

> Recite in the Book the account of Mary, when she withdrew from her people to a place towards the east; and drew a curtain, screening herself from people whereupon We sent to her Our spirit and he appeared to her as a well-shaped man. Mary exclaimed: "I surely take refuge from you with the Most Compassionate Lord, if you are at all God-fearing." He said: "I am just a message-bearer of your Lord, I have come to grant you a most pure boy." Mary said: "How can a boy be born to me when no man has even touched me, nor have I ever been unchaste?" The angel said: "Thus shall it be. Your Lord says: 'It is easy for Me; and We shall do so in order to make him a Sign for mankind and a mercy from Us. This has been decreed.'"

> Then she conceived him and withdrew with him to a far-off place. Then the birth pangs drove her to the trunk of a palm-tree and she said: "Oh, would that I had died before this and had been all forgotten." Thereupon the angel below her cried out: "Grieve not, for your Lord has caused a stream of water to flow beneath you. Shake the trunk of the palm-tree towards yourself and fresh and ripe dates shall fall upon you. So eat and drink and cool your eyes; and if you see any person say to him: 'Verily I have vowed a fast to the Most Compassionate Lord, and so I shall not speak to anyone today.'" Then she came to her people, carrying her baby. They said: "O Mary! You have committed a monstrous thing. O sister of Aaron! Your father was not an evil man, nor was your mother an unchaste woman." Thereupon, Mary pointed to the child. They exclaimed: "How can we speak to one who is in the cradle, a mere child?" The child cried out: "Verily I am Allah's servant. He has granted me the Book and has made me a Prophet and has blessed me wherever I might be and has enjoined upon me prayer and charity as long as I live; and has made me dutiful to my mother. He has not made me oppressive, nor bereft of God's blessings. Peace be upon me the day I was born and the day I will die, and the day I will be raised up alive." This is Jesus, son of Mary; and this is the truth about him concerning which they are in doubt. It does not befit God to take for Himself a son. Glory be to Him! When He decrees a thing He only says: 'Be' and it is.[51]

The verse clearly states that ʿĪsā was the servant of God and the son of Maryam. God created him without a father similar to Adam who was created without both parents. His mother devoted herself to worship in an eastern corner of the al-Aqṣā Mosque. It also mentions that Maryam experiences the pain of childbirth far

[51] Qur'ān 19: 16-34.

from her people and family, close to a palm trunk, and that 'Īsā was born in the summer during the harvesting of dates.

The land where 'Īsā was born was a land of palm trees in the far east, which has to be far from Bethlehem, which is south of Jerusalem and not a place of palm trees. It is perhaps in eastern Jerusalem closer to Jericho, which is known since ancient times for its palm trees.

The Mosque of 'Umar

We left the church and walked towards the Mosque of 'Umar b. al-Khaṭṭāb, the oldest mosque in the city of Bethlehem, located in the plain of the Nativity near the church. Mosques attributed to 'Umar or the other Rightly-Guided Caliphs are numerous throughout the world. The people of Bethlehem claim that this mosque was built to commemorate the visit of 'Umar after he had issued a decree guaranteeing safety for all Christians and clerics and respect for their holy places. It was rebuilt by the Jordanian authorities in 1955.

The mosque consists of three floors, with the upper containing the prayer space, the middle including a water fountain and facilities of the Islamic court, and the lower grounds containing shops. In the front of the mosque directly outside the door stand two massive palm trees.

Our return to Jerusalem

When we came out of Bethlehem, we encountered a great crowd. The soldiers were thoroughly searching every vehicle entering Jerusalem. We were dismayed and shocked to witness the fear that was ever-present in them. What a barbaric people that continue to frustrate the lives of people. What a pity at our utter weakness and ineptitude that these calamities have become so commonplace that we appear to expect them or even welcome them. We have become accustomed to injustice and injury, settling for humiliation and disgrace. When calamities and heavy losses continue to raid a people, then what critics have to say is meaningless.

We arrived back at the hotel at 7:00 pm. After resting a bit, we broke our fasts at the hotel and prayed Tarawīḥ in the mosque. I went to sleep thinking about the catastrophe that the inhabitants of Palestine have had to endure. Not equal were the great morals of a people who emerged from the tree of faith and piety, with the propaganda and claims of those who come out of shrubs and foliage. My tears welled up and began to flow. Know that those whose tears flow not over injustice become part of injustice themselves.

CITY WALLS

4

CITY WALLS

Wednesday 21st Ramadan 1436 AH

After having our morning meal and praying the Fajr prayer in the mosque, we rested until 8:00 am. Today was the day we visit al-Aqṣā Mosque and its surrounding historical sites.

City Walls

We started by exploring the city walls, which were built—as previously mentioned—by Sulaymān the Magnificent. There are eleven doors, and seven of them are open: Bāb al-Khalīl, or Jaffa Gate, on the western wall; Bāb al-Jadīd, also known as the gate of Sulṭān ʿAbd al-Ḥamīd II on the northern side; Bāb al-ʿUmūd, or the Damascus Gate, in the middle of the northern wall; Bāb al-Sāhirah, or Herod's Gate, in the northern wall; Bāb al-Maghāribah, or Moroccan Gate, in the south-western side; Bāb al-Nabī Dāwūd, or Zion Gate, on the southern wall; and Bāb al-Aswad, or Lions Gate in the eastern wall.

The four closed doors are Bāb al-Raḥmah 200 meters south of the Lions Gate, Bāb al-Mufrad in the southern wall near the south-eastern corner, and Bāb al-Thulāthī (Triple Gate) and Bāb al-Mazdūj (Double Gate) at the southern wall.

We entered the city from Bāb al-Sāhirah, with the Damascus Gate to our right at a distance of half a kilometer. This was our entrance towards the hotel. It is a small door that is richly decorated and leads to the neighborhood of Saʿdiyah and Bāb al-Ḥiṭṭah. The word *sāhirah* means a flat and spacious place, and in common vernacular became changed to *zāhirah*, and ultimately to *zahūr*.

King Faisal Gate

We walked through the old city streets and entered the mosque through the door of King Faisal to the right of the Ḥiṭṭah Gate (Forgiveness Gate). At the door were posted guards of the Jewish state performing security searches. This door is known by several names; The most famous of which is the Gate of Darkness (Bab al-ʿAtam), named after the construction of the archway to the north caused darkness in broad daylight. The door is also known as the Honorable Prophets Gate (Bāb Sharaf al-Anbiyā') and, more recently, as King Faisal Gate in honor of King Faisal II of Iraq who visited in 1943 and contributed towards the renovation of al-Aqṣā Mosque.

We entered the mosque at about 10:30 am, and the first thing we noticed were two old men fighting with each other quite intensely.

Temple of Solomon

Many Jews have popularized the myth of Solomon's Temple, claiming that it was the first Jewish temple built by King Solomon which was destroyed by Nebuchadnezzar II after the siege of Jerusalem in 587 BC. They presume that its location is the site of the Dome of the Rock or close to it, but many historians and archaeologists believe that the story of the temple is fabricated.

Dome of the Rock

Around 11:00 am we entered the Dome of the Rock's prayer hall, which was built by the Caliph ʿAbd al-Malik b. Marwān as an octagonal building with four doors. Inside, there is another octagon built upon columns and pillars. From there, we descended under the Rock into a cave with an old niche (miḥrāb) referred to as the prayer space of prophets.

We were accompanied by an official guide who was relating to us many nonsensical and false tales, such as the claim that 'Abd al-Malik b. Marwān built the rock so that people would divert the pilgrimage of Makkah to this place instead and that the rock is from Paradise and suspended between heaven and earth. He also claimed that it bears the imprint of the footsteps of the Prophet and the fingers of the angels. I was forced to quietly inform my companions that the guide was relating lies and fabrications.

Old Mosque

We performed ablution at the lower fountain at around 11:30 am. The restrooms and fountains were exceptionally clean. We entered the ground floor of the al-Aqṣā Mosque through a stone staircase. This was the old mosque, consisting of two large galleries. Here, we prayed two rak'ahs of prayer. It is said that this was built by 'Umar. It has a place for lamps and oils, and contains huge stone columns reportedly constructed by the Prophet Sulaymān, peace be upon him.

The Library

We entered from the old mosque to the Khataniyyah Library, which is a large library constructed by Ṣalāh al-Dīn and entrusted to Shaykh Jalāl al-Dīn Aḥmad b. Aḥmad b. Muḥammad al-Shāsh on the 18th Rabī' al-Awwal 587 AH. A large number of senior and prominent scholars have taught here since. In 1999, it underwent significant renovations. It is named after Shaykh 'Abdullah of Hotan (Khutan), in the greater Turkistān region, who visited in its early days. The library represents an ancient museum that preserves rare and valuable manuscripts.

The Wailing Wall

We exited the mosque from Bāb al-Silsilah at 12:15 pm and headed over towards the Western Wall. After passing through inspections we finally reached the wall, which is a famous visitation site where those of the Jewish faith weep and mourn.

Muslims refer to it as the Wall of Burrāq claiming that the Messenger of God, peace be upon him, tied his animal here during the night journey. The mosque borders are on the western side and run from the Moroccan Gate to the south until north of the Tankazī School.[52] At a length of fifty meters and a height of roughly forty meters, it is called the Wailing Wall because the Jews believe that this wall is the only surviving remnant of the Temple of Solomon and that it is forbidden for them to enter the mosque since the destruction of the temple. They consider this wall to be the direction of their prayers and perform the rituals of prayer and mourning in front of it. Among those rituals is to display remorse and grief at their displacement and humiliation in the land. This tradition of wailing at this site goes back to the Ottoman era.

Moroccan Gate

Next, we visited the Moroccan Gate from where it is said the Prophet, peace be upon him, entered the mosque. We entered the hall next to the gate and found a large number of Jews reading the Torah. It is named so because visitors coming from Morocco would cross it to visit al-Aqṣā Mosque.

Conversation with some Jews

We spoke at the Wailing Wall near the Moroccan Gate with a number of Jews about the current situation in Palestine. I had a discussion with one of them about the claim that the Qur'ān orders the killing of all Jews, and that even trees speak of the same. I simply said to him, "Look, copies of the Qur'ān are readily available in all

---

[52] Mamlūk-era school in Jerusalem.

languages, so why don't you obtain one in your own language and read it for yourself? Your problem is that you rely only on reports and rumors." I then asked him if the Torah ordered the killing of all Muslims. He replied, "No." I asked him, "Then why are Jews killing Muslims, destroying their livelihood and sowing turmoil in God's land?" He was silent after that.

Church of the Holy Sepulchre

Then we went through ancient roads and old buildings to the Mosque of 'Umar passing by the Church of the Holy Sepulchre. It was built by a Byzantine princess above Golgotha, the site where it was believed Jesus was crucified. It was rebuilt by Crusaders who fabricated a story that this is the tomb of Jesus that should be visited. It was also named the Church of the Resurrection because it was believed that Jesus rose from here. Of course, this is a falsehood, as God states in the Qur'ān: "*And they did not kill him, nor did they crucify him; but [another] was made to resemble him to them. And indeed, those who differ over it are in doubt about it. They have no knowledge of it except the following of assumption. And they did not kill him, for certain, but God raised him up.*"[53]

Mosque of 'Umar b. al-Khaṭṭāb

We entered the mosque of 'Umar b. al- Khaṭṭāb around 1:15 pm. It is located in the southern courtyard of the Church of the Holy Sepulchre. When the second Caliph 'Umar conquered Jerusalem, he accepted the invitation of the Patriarch[54] to come here. When the prayer time came, 'Umar asked the Patriarch where he could perform his prayers. He replied, "This place is yours, so pray here." 'Umar refused, fearing that Muslims would take over this place on the pretext that 'Umar had prayed here. So he walked away to a slightly farther place, put down his cloak and performed his

[53] Qur'ān 4:157.

[54] The Patriarch was Sophronius, now venerated as a saint, who served as the Patriarch of Jerusalem from 634 until his death in 638 CE.

prayers. Later, a mosque was built on this place. It was shaped into its present form by Afḍal, the son of Ṣalāḥ al-Dīn in 1193 CE, and renovated by the Ottoman Sulṭān ʿAbd al-Majīd I, who reigned from 1839—1860.

On the mosque wall, the following is written:

> In the name of God, the Merciful, the Compassionate. This is the assurance of safety [*amān*] which the servant of God ʿUmar, the Commander of the Faithful, has given to the people of Jerusalem. He has given them an assurance of safety for themselves, for their property, their churches, their crosses, the sick and healthy of the city and for all the rituals which belong to their religion. Their churches will not be inhabited by Muslims and will not be destroyed. Neither they, nor the land on which they stand, nor their cross, nor their property will be damaged. They will not be forcibly converted. No Jew will live with them in Jerusalem. The people of Jerusalem must pay the taxes (*jizya*) like the people of other cities and must expel the Byzantines and the robbers. Those of the people of Jerusalem who want to leave with the Byzantines, take their property and abandon their churches and crosses will be safe until the reach their place of refuge. The villagers [*ahl al-ard*, who had taken refuge in the city at the time of the conquest] may remain in the city if they wish but must pay taxes like the citizens. Those who wish may go with the Byzantines and those who wish may return to their families. Nothing is to be taken from them before their harvest is reaped. If they pay their taxes according to their obligations, then the conditions laid out in this letter are under the covenant of God, are the responsibility of His Prophet, of the caliphs and of the faithful.[55]

[55] This pact is known as *al-ʿUhdah al-ʿUmariyyah* and was issued to the people of Aelia, the Roman name for Jerusalem. For the Arabic text, see Pg. 102. Muḥammad al-Khuḍarī Beg. *Itmām al-Wafāʾ fī Sīrat al-Khulafāʾ*. The English

This letter was written in 15/637. Historians have differed greatly over the narration of the text of this treaty, but this is not the place for this discussion. I led the Ẓuhr prayer and delivered a talk about the history of Jerusalem, followed by answering some questions. We left the mosque at 2:00 pm passing through several shops and markets.

Ṣalāḥiyyah Khānqah

We then walked to the Ṣalāḥiyyah Khānqah[56] which is on the other side of the Church of the Holy Sepulchre. It was endowed by Ṣalāḥ al-Dīn in 583/1187. We went through the large entrance leading to an open corridor and arrived at the massive ground floor. It is said that this is where Ṣalāḥ al-Dīn would stay. The building consists of a dining hall and a military training center.

It is now inhabited by some private residents while the Khānqah remains closed. The land is now divided between an active mosque and school called al-Hudā School. We then took the stone staircase leading us to the second floor where there are a number of halls and rooms, an inscription on a marble plaque bearing the name of the founder ʿĪsa b. Aḥmad b. Ghānim and the date of construction: 741/1340.

Ṣalāḥī Hospital

We left the Khānqah at 2:30 pm and passed by Ṣalāḥī Hospital, also known as the Mauristan,[57] to the west of the al-Aqṣā Mosque. This was established by Ṣalāḥ al-Dīn in 583/1187 as a great endowment in which he appointed some of the most famous doctors of his time.

---

translation is from pg 91-2, Kennedy. *The Great Arab Conquests: How the Spread of Islām Changed the World We Live In.*

[56] A khanqah, also known as a zāwiyah, is a term used to denote the physical lodges and seminaries in the Muslim world which served as centres for spiritual retreat used by those who participated in the spiritual path known as taṣawwuf (Sufism).

[57] From a Persian word for hospital: māristān or bīmāristān.

Medicine was also taught here. It consists of an open courtyard surrounded by bungalows of stone pillars and staves. These bungalows have multiple halls of varying sizes, with each designated for a specific medical specialization such as ophthalmology and gastroenterology. The hospital was well-known during the reign of Ṣalāḥ al-Dīn, and in the later years, for treating wounded and sick soldiers as well as the general population. It also distributed medicines and drugs to the people free of charge. In fact, Palestine and the rest of the Levant is full of testimony to the great work done by Ṣalāḥ al-Dīn for the region.

A brother's touch and father's care
Along with mother's love
The rare person who joins all these
Among all ranks he's far above.
Because of him I do forget
The other kin that I have lost.[58]

Back to al-Aqṣā Mosque

We finally returned to al-Aqṣā Mosque and encountered guards at the gate who were only allowing entry to those whom they were certain happened to be Muslim. In our group there was a woman who had recently embraced Islam, which made the guards suspicious. They asked her to recite sūrah al-Fātiḥah,[59] which she did and so, they allowed her in.

Bāb al-Raḥmah

We left to see Bāb al-Raḥmah, one of the permanently closed gates in the eastern wall which is located inside a tall building that can be seen from inside al-Aqṣā. It is comprised of two gates: Bāb al-Raḥmah on the south and Bāb al-Tawbah on the north. These

[58] Pg. 337. Abū Tamām. *Dīwān al-Ḥamāsah.*

[59] The first and most important chapter of the Qur'ān since it is recited in each prayer.

were built in the reign of 'Abd al-Malik b. Marwān as evidenced by its architectural and artistic elements. The door remained open until the crusaders invaded and entered the mosque, massacring and torturing a large number of Muslims. As a result, Ṣalāḥ al-Dīn had the gate permanently closed in order to protect the city and mosque from the barbarians.

Zāwiyah of Imam Ghazali

We passed through the Zāwiyah[60] of Imām Abū Ḥāmid Ghazālī (d. 505/1111), in which rests the upper portion of Bāb al-Raḥmah. The renowned Imām used to teach in al-Aqṣā Mosque and this is where he authored his famous work Iḥyā' 'Ulūm al-Dīn ('The Revival of the Religious Sciences). The zāwiyah is in a larger square called Ghazālī Square. It also houses the shrine of Sulaymān and the Jinn Prison which is under the wall.

The Cemetery of Bāb al-Raḥmah

We emerged from Lions Gate to the cemetery of Bāb al-Raḥmah, which starts at the eastern wall of the mosque and extends through Lions Gate to the end of the wall close to the Ummayad palaces in the south. We visited the grave of the Companion 'Ubādah b. Ṣāmit (d. 34 AH) and Abū Ya'lā Shaddād b. Aws b. Thābit al-Anṣārī who lived in Jerusalem and died in 58 AH. We visited the graves of many warriors who were involved in the conquests of Jerusalem during the reins of 'Umar and Ṣalāḥ al-Dīn. We recited al-Fātiḥah and prayed for them and ourselves.

I swear by life their graves conceal
gripping palms on aged spears
And all the good that I have seen
Reminds me of their lofty deeds
And with the evil all around
Their clash and skirmish I still see.[61]

[60] See previous footnote 56.
[61] Pg. 190. Abū Tamām. *Dīwān al-Ḥamāsah.*

The Cradle of Mary

Then we went to Church of Saint Anne which is said to be the location of the birth of Maryam, peace be upon her, and was built by Crusaders in 1138 CE. In 1192 CE, several years after the liberation of Jerusalem, it was turned into the Ṣalāḥīyyah School, with the name being engraved on the school entrance. The school occupied a huge intellectual position in Jerusalem.

We went back to the hotel a little before 4:00 pm to take some rest. Afterwards, I recited some Qur'ān and asked my daughter to review her Arabic lessons. We broke our fast in the restaurant of the hotel and prayed Maghrib in the hotel. Today would be a lecture by Shaykh Abū Sneina to the group after Tarawīḥ prayer.

Talk by Shaykh Abū Sneina

Shaykh Yūsuf Abū Sneina, Imām of al-Aqṣā Mosque visited us at the hotel after Tarawīḥ prayers and delivered a speech starting well after midnight. He said the following:

> I am very happy to see Muslims from the United Kingdom visiting the al-Aqṣā Mosque, because this mosque is not for the Arabs alone, but belongs to all Muslims. They should visit it frequently. The Prophet, peace be upon him, said: "Do not undertake a journey to visit any mosque, but three: this mosque of mine, the Mosque of al-Ḥarām and the Mosque of al-Aqṣā."[62] I do not know why many Muslims limit their visits to the other two Holy Mosques while leaving out al-Aqṣā, even though we are under occupation and want you to help us through your visits. The Messenger of God, peace be upon him, undertook his night journey to here (al-Isrā) and ascended to the heavens from here (al-Mi'rāj). And it was the first qiblah for Muslims.

[62] Bukhārī and Muslim. See footnote 45.

'Umar arrived in Jerusalem in the year 15 AH and came down from Mount Mukabbar. It was named thus because he said while climbing it: "God is great! (Allāhu Akbar)." No less than four thousand companions were known to have entered the city. 'Ubādah b. Ṣāmit was its first teacher and judge. Then came the Crusaders in 492 AH who killed 70,000 people. The city was later liberated by Ṣalāḥ al-Dīn after a period of ninety years. It remained under Muslim control until the British colonized it for thirty-five years.[63] It was finally occupied in 1948. The situation here is as bad as it can be. They have closed everything to Muslims in Jerusalem. There are no jobs for us or for our children. They are always thinking of new ways to displace more Arabs from here. We are pleased by your visit from Britain, and we ask you to visit us in times apart from Ramadan as well, for these visits provide great support for your brothers in Jerusalem and the rest of Palestine

We remain steadfast in the face of conspiracies and calamities and call upon God to strengthen our resolve, make us steadfast and grant us tremendous help.

[63] The British, led by General Edmund Allenby, entered Jerusalem after Turkish troops left on December 11, 1917, and remained until May 1948.

TEACHING IN THE HOLY LAND

5

TEACHING IN THE HOLY LAND

Thursday 22nd Ramadan 1436 AH

After having our morning meal at the hotel, I met with Zayd, who gifted me a book titled *Atlas of the al-Aqṣā Mosque* written by Dr. ʿAbdullah ʿUmar and Rifʿat Marʿī. Afterwards, we prayed Fajr in the mosque together and then I returned to rest. Today would be a full day of teaching.

Lesson on Seeking Knowledge

Today I was scheduled to teach a class at 3:15 pm in the dining hall. I came down at around 3:00 pm and found it full of students. I taught the class based on Shaykh ʿAbd al-Fattāḥ Abū Ghuddah's[64] book *Ṣafaḥāt min Ṣabr al-ʿUlamā'*[65] ('Pages from the Diligence of the Scholars'). I began by reminding everyone that our religion is based upon sound and established evidences, which must be learned properly. This can only be realized through sustained effort and constant struggle, just as all good virtues are attained only by persistent practice and serious resolve.

I acquainted them with the subject-matter of the book as well as its author, while providing specific examples of the sacrifices of early Muslims for the sake of knowledge. I began with the story of Adam, as narrated by Bukhārī and Muslim, that the Prophet, peace be upon him, said:

---

[64] He is the renowned Syrian ḥadīth scholar and writer who was one of Shaykh Akram Nadwī's senior teachers. He died in 1417/1997 at the age of 79.
[65] Aleppo: Maktabah Al-Maṭbūʿāt al-Islāmiyyah. 1394/1974.

> After God had created Adam, He said to him, "Go and greet that group of angels sitting there, and listen what they will say in reply to you, for that will be your greeting and the greeting of your offspring." Adam (went and) said, *'al-salāmu 'alaykum'* ('peace be upon you'). They replied, *'al-salāmu 'alayka wa raḥmatullāh'* ('peace and God's mercy be on you'). So they had increased *'wa raḥmatullāh'*.[66]

I also mentioned the Qur'ānic story of the creation of Adam and Eve, and the journey of Mūsā to Khiḍr even though God had already chosen Mūsā for His message and His service, and drawn him near. Mūsā's attaining the highest position of leadership did not prevent him from traveling over land and sea for the sake of knowledge. Some scholars have said, "What Mūsā endured in terms of hardship, travel, patience and humility before Khiḍr, and his singularity of purpose—despite possessing a high rank with God as well as the mantle of prophethood—is proof for the great rank of knowledge and its seekers, and the virtue of humility towards those who seek it and those from whom it is learned."

I told them about the struggle of the four Muḥammads during their studies in Egypt. Abū al-'Abbās al-Bakrī, who was from the descendants of Abū Bakr al-Ṣiddīq, writes:

> I recorded the journey of Muḥammad b. Jarīr (Ṭabarī), Muḥammad b. Isḥāq b. Khuzaymah (Ibn Khuzaymah), Muḥammad b. Naṣr al-Marwazī, and Muḥammad b. Hārūn al-Rūyyānī in Egypt. They had little food and frequently remained hungry. Once, they gathered in a house where they used to stay and decided to draw lots. Whoever's name was drawn would look for food on behalf of everyone else.
>
> The name of Muḥammad b. Isḥāq b. Khuzaymah was drawn. He asked his companions to give him some time

[66] Ṣaḥīḥ Bukhārī: Kitāb aḥādīth al-anbiyā'—Bāb khalq Ādam; Kitāb al-isti'dhān—Bāb bad' al-islām.

> to pray first. He performed ablution and began to pray. While engrossed in prayer, someone knocked on the door. When they opened the door, it was the governor of Egypt.
>
> He came off his mount and asked, "Which one of you is Muḥammad b. Naṣr? He came forward. The governor took out a money bag containing fifty dīnārs and gave it to him. Then he asked, "Which one of you is Muḥammad b. Jarīr? He came forward. The governor took out a money bag containing fifty dīnārs and gave it to him. He then asked, "Which one of you is Muḥammad b. Hārūn? He came forward. The governor took out a money bag containing fifty dīnārs and gave it to him. Finally, he asked "Which one of you is Muḥammad b. Isḥāq b. Khuzaymah?" They responded, "He is praying." When he finished and came forward, the governor took out a money bag containing fifty dīnārs and gave it to him, saying: "The ruler saw a dream yesterday and commanded us: 'The Muḥammads are overtaken by hunger. I am giving you these pouches to distribute to them. If you happen to run out, I will give you more.'"

I also mentioned other stories from the book to inspire vigor, resolve and determination to study and sacrifice. I then answered questions. One of them was about the creation of women. I explained to them that men and women are both created from one soul. They are both created independently and are equal in receiving commands and prohibitions, and in obedience, repentance to God and forgiveness. I cited Qur'ānic verses as proofs. I was also asked about the meaning of the verse: "I have chosen you for my service."[67] There was another question on whether God had sent prophets to the people of India, China and other countries that are not mentioned in the Holy Qur'an.

---

[67] Qur'ān 20:41.

Lecture on Death

Afterwards, we went to pray the ʿAṣr prayer at the Qiblī Mosque. We explored the Marwānī prayer hall, which is located below the southeast corner of the al-Aqṣā Mosque. This portion was formerly known as the 'eastern settlement' since it was built by the Umayyads originally as an architectural settlement on the original mount of Jerusalem, descending to the south. The reason for its construction was so there could be a building built above its southern section closest to the Qibla on flat ground that would make it rise to the level of the northern section. The Marwānī prayer hall consists of sixteen rooms, and its total area covers more than four dunams.[68] It is the largest covered area for prayer at al-Aqṣā.

When we entered the Marwānī hall, we found it filled with a large number of people engaged in iʿtikāf,[69] including some of my own students from the United Kingdom. We moved to the other side of the hall, where I began my lecture by answering questions first. Questions included the love of God for Mūsā, and the meaning of the verse 'Men are caretakers of women.'[70]

The lesson now was from the Book of Remembering Death from Imām Ghazālī's Iḥyā' 'Ulūm al-Dīn. I started by providing them with a short summary of the life of the great Imām and then the definition of the term *iḥyā'* ('revival'). I also mentioned that the book contained some weaknesses on account of some unfounded interpretations of the Qur'ān as well as the presence of many weak, and even fabricated, ḥadīth narrations. Students should be on guard for these things, and not accept anything that was not based on sound evidences and clear proofs.

I then explained to them the meaning of the verse: "*Say that the death you flee from will surely meet you*;"[71] the ḥadīth of the Prophet, peace be upon him: "Remember frequently the destroyer of

---

[68] See footnote 21.

[69] Religious seclusion in the mosque usually practiced in Ramadan.

[70] Qur'ān 4:34.

[71] Qur'ān 62:8.

pleasures: death."[72]; and the statement of Ḥasan al-Baṣrī: "Death has disgraced this world." I acquainted them with Ḥasan al-Baṣrī and his keen understanding of religion. I also mentioned some other things related to remembering death.

The reality is that death is the real end of every living being and the clearest, most certain of all matters. Annihilation exists very close to existence itself. And God destroys false hopes and delusions. When any people begin to enjoy their lives in their homes and lands, drowning themselves in pleasures and desires, the decree is issued for their annihilation. We must look at our lives are as if we are all heading towards the cemetery with our families and friends, carrying our own biers to the pits which we dig with our own hands to pour dirt over ourselves.

Destroyer of pleasures, there is no escape or refuge from you! Our souls continue to warn us about you and the calamities you are bringing towards us. We have experienced your lessons and warnings at the archaeological remains and ruins that speak of their past. We have heard moving reminders about you, if only we were moved! We read verses from the Book about you, if only we benefited from them! Every soul will get what it strived for. Every soul has an appointment on a day that will never be hastened nor delayed in the least.

I answered questions, one of which was: If the Qur'ān and Sunnah are two primary sources we have to follow, then does that not impose difficulties upon us, as our context is different from the context of the past? Doesn't wisdom dictate that different circumstances and conditions be taken into consideration? I replied: Of course, the commands of the Qur'ān and Sunnah are inclusive of the consideration for context and circumstance. So the sīrah (holistic life of the Prophet, peace be upon him) is the context for the Sunnah, so that must be studied in order to understand the

---

[72] Related by Tirmidhī, Ibn Mājah and al-Nasā'ī, and authenticated by Ibn Ḥibbān.

Sunnah's historical context. So there are three basic elements: first, the Qur'ānic education; and second, the Prophetic application of that, which basically represents the first application of the Qur'ān and is found in the Sunnah and sīrah; and finally, there is our own application, which is the new application of Qur'ānic principles by each Muslim into his/her own life according to his/her own peculiar circumstances and conditions guided by Prophetic guidance.

The lesson ended at 6:30 pm and we returned to the hotel in order to rest and get ready for breaking our fast.

Lesson on the Descent of Jesus

Today, I would be scheduled for another talk after 'Ishā' and Tarawīḥ prayers, this time designated for the general public. We arrived in the shaded area next to the Dome of the Rock and found Imām Yūsuf Abū Sneina walking towards us. I asked him to deliver the lesson in my place, and he agreed.

His lesson was on the Dajjāl (the Antichrist), descent of 'Īsā, and appearance of the Mahdī. He started by mentioning that the ḥadīth reports concerning the Mahdī are mass-transmitted,[73] and that 'Īsā would pray behind Imām Mahdī in the al-Aqṣā mosque. He also said that 'Īsā would descend in the eastern minaret in Damascus and make his way to Jerusalem. Here, he would come to al-Aqṣā mosque from the Mount of Olives and enter from the Gate of Mercy and pray two rak'ah. He would then proceed towards the gate of Lod[74] where he would kill the Antichrist. He also mentioned that the Antichrist is currently present somewhere on a deserted island in the sea, citing the ḥadīth of Tamīm al-Dārī.

I personally have some disagreements concerning what he told us about the reports of the Mahdī being mass-transmitted and some of the details concerning 'Īsā, but this is not the place for that.

---

[73] *Mutawātir.*

[74] Ancient Biblical city in Israel.

Exhausting Walk

After the lesson, we exited through Bāb Ḥiṭṭah, which was our gateway back to the hotel. We found it to be closed, so we were forced to use Bāb al-Silsilah which was exhaustingly far. We were trying to avoid the Jewish quarters, whose streets are overly crowded even at late night. We did not arrive at our beds until being fully exhausted by the walking and effort.

GREAT CROWDS

6

GREAT CROWDS

Friday 23rd Ramadan 1436 AH

Today, al-Aqṣā Mosque would witness massive crowds coming from all over Palestine to perform Friday prayers, with total numbers expected to exceed half a million or more. Imām Yūsuf Abū Sneina advised us to leave the hotel well before 10:00 am. However, I was daunted to leave so early on account of my fatigue.

Pre-Adhān Sermon

Sermons here are delivered by imāms before the call to prayer, and we wanted to attend at least one prior to returning home. We entered the mosque from King Faisal Gate around 12:00 pm, and could not find any space except in the Ghazālī Square. The Imām was warning people from falling into prohibition and sin, citing the story of people of Ṭālūt who had disobeyed him:

> *And when Saul went forth with the soldiers, he said, 'Indeed, God will be testing you with a river. So, whoever drinks from it is not of me, and whoever does not taste it is indeed of me, excepting one who takes [from it] in the hollow of his hand.' But they drank from it, except a [very] few of them. Then when he had crossed it along with those who believed with him, they said, 'There is no power for us today against Goliath and his soldiers.' But those who were certain that they would meet God said, 'How many a small company has overcome a large company by permission of God. And God is with the patient.'*[75]

---

[75] Qur'ān 2:249.

He also shared the story of Yūsuf, highlighting his chastity, purity and patience as the princess and other women sought to seduce him in the prime of his youth. He remained fearful of God and controlled his own self. The Imām spoke about the meaning of the verse: "*so that He might mark out those who fear Him, even though He is beyond the reach of human perception.*"[76]

He also related the story of Abū Masʿūd from Ṣaḥīḥ Muslim, who narrated:

> I was beating my slave with a whip when I heard a voice behind me: "Understand, Abū Masʿūd!" However, I did not recognize the voice due to my state of anger. As he came near me, I saw that he was God's Messenger, peace be upon him, who kept saying: "Understand, Abū Masʿūd! Understand, Abū Masʿūd!" I threw the whip from my hand. Thereupon he said: "Bear in mind, Abū Masʿūd, that God surely has more power and dominance over you than you have upon your slave." I then said: "I would never beat my servant in the future again."[77]

He also said: God is surely All-Powerful and the Owner of Retribution. "*Surely forgiveness and a mighty reward await those who fear God without seeing Him.*"[78] I pray that God make us from those who listen to speech and then follow the best of it. I pray that He make us from those whose worship is accepted in the month of Ramadan. I ask that He make our insides better than our exteriors. I pray that He rectify the state of the Muslim ummah and the Muslim youth around the world, accept our deeds and bring Ramadan back to us again while we are in a better state of affairs.

---

76 Qur'ān 5:94.

77 Ṣaḥīḥ Muslim: Kitāb al-īmān—Bāb ṣuḥbat al-mamālīk wa kaffārat man laṭama ʿabdahū.

78 Qur'ān 67:12.

Then another Imām spoke about the virtues of al-Aqṣā Mosque, saying: "It is the first qiblah, the second of the two mosques, and the third of the sacred sanctuaries."

Actually, the final portion is not correct. Al-Aqṣā Mosque is indeed the third of the three mosques that one is permitted to travel to (for a religious journey), but there are only two sacred sanctuaries in Islam: Makkah and Madīnah.

Then the imām extolled the virtues of the Prophet, peace be upon him, endowed upon him by God, saying:

Oh best of those who live
Within the best of grounds
Delightful one who spreads his charms
beneath, above the ground
without a second thought I would
ransom this soul of mine
for this exalted grave you fill
with grace of every kind.[79]

All this time, we were sitting in the open sun in Ghazālī Square. A team came and began spraying water over people in order to protect them from the excessive heat.

The imām moved on to speak about the great Follower and one of the renowned 'seven jurists of Madīnah' Sa'īd b. al-Musayyab. He related his virtues from sources such as Dhahabī's Siyar and others. He mentioned the story of the marriage of his daughter to a pious man. None other than the Caliph 'Abd al-Malik Marwān had proposed to her on behalf of his son Walīd, but Sa'īd had refused. The ruler continued to persist, even to the point of punishing Sa'īd with a hundred lashes on a cold day, then pouring cold water on him and forcing him to wear a woolen cloak.

---

[79] These verses were supposedly composed by a Bedouin Arab at the grave of the Prophet, as related by Bayhaqī in Shu'b al-Īmān and others with an extremely weak isnād. See pg. 766-7, Ibn Taymiyyah. *Iqtiḍā' al-Ṣirāṭ al-Mustaqīm*.

Kathīr b. Abī Wadā'ah states: I used to sit in Sa'īd's assemblies, and once, I happened to miss them for a number of days. When I returned, he asked me where I was. I replied that my wife had died and I was busy with that. He asked me why I didn't inform him so that he could have attended the funeral. Later, he asked me: "Have you found a new wife?" I replied: "God have mercy on you. Who would marry me when I only possess two or three dirhams?" Sa'īd responded: "Marry my daughter." I asked: "Would she agree to that?" He responded: "Yes." So he conducted the marriage contract with two or three dirhams as dowry. I went home that day and began to think of who I could borrow from in order to conduct a celebration. I prayed Maghrib in the mosque and returned home. I lived alone and had been fasting. I began to prepare a meal, and all I had was bread and oil. Then someone knocked on the door. I asked: "Who is it?" He responded: "Sa'īd." I began to think of all the Sa'īds I knew except for Sa'īd b. al-Musayyab, because he was someone who for forty years was only seen between his house and the mosque. I came out and found it was Sa'īd b. al-Musayyab, or someone resembling him—or so I thought. When I realized it was him, I said: "O Abū Muḥammad, why didn't you send for me, so I could have come to you?" Sa'īd responded: "Rather it is your right that I come to you. You are a bachelor who just got married, and I hated that you should spend a single night alone. Here is your wife!" And his daughter was standing right behind him, hidden behind his length. Sa'īd took her hand, led her inside and closed the door and left. She nearly fainted out of shyness and stayed by the door. I hid my food bowl behind the lamp so she would not see it. I came to the roof of my house and called my neighbors. I informed them of my marriage so they could come down and meet her. The news reached my mother immediately. She came and said to me, "My face is forbidden for you if you touch her before I get her ready for three days." After three days, I finally saw her, and she was one of the most beautiful of all people. She was also the most knowledgeable of people in the Qur'ān and the Sunnah of the

God's Messenger, peace be upon him. She was also the most aware of people concerning the rights of the husband.

He concluded by supplicating and sending blessings on the Prophet, peace be upon him, and then reciting the verse: "*But for those whom We had decided to favor with good reward, they shall be kept far removed from Hell. They shall not hear even a whisper of it, and they shall live forever in the delights which they had desired.*"[80]

Friday Sermon

The first adhān was called at 12:45 pm after which Shaykh 'Ikrimah 'Abdullah Ṣabrī sat on the pulpit and greeted the audience. Born in 1939, he is the muftī of Jerusalem and Palestine. After the second adhān, Shaykh 'Ikrimah stood up and began his sermon:

> Praise be to God who allowed us to reach the month of Ramadan and blessed us with fasting and prayer. Bukhārī and Muslim relate from Abū Hurairah that the Messenger of God said, "God the Exalted and Majestic says: 'Every act of the son of Adam is for him, except for fasting, which is exclusively for Me, and I will reward him for it.' Fasting is a shield. When anyone of you is observing fasting, he should neither indulge in obscene language nor should he raise his voice; and if anyone reviles him or tries to quarrel with him, he should respond: 'I am fasting.' By the One in Whose Hand is the soul of Muḥammad, the breath of the fasting one is sweeter to God than the fragrance of musk. The one who fasts, experiences two joys: at the breaking of his fast and when he meets his Lord."[81]
>
> This is the fourth Friday of the blessed month of Ramadan in the blessed al-Aqṣā Mosque, whose surroundings God has blessed.

---

[80] Qur'ān 21:101-2.

[81] Ṣaḥīḥ Bukhārī: Kitāb al-Tawḥīd—Bāb qawl Allāh: yurīdūna an yubaddilū kalām Allāh.

The imām welcomed those coming from all over Palestine and said: "All of you are affiliated with the al-Aqṣā Mosque through your faith" and mentioned the story of the night journey and ascension (Isrā' and Mi'rāj). He said, "Your association with the mosque is firstly through your creed, and secondly, through your worship, for prayer here has multifold rewards. How about if you add fasting to that? It is also one of the mosques that is the destination of religious journeys. This is the holy mosque to which believers aspire to, despite hardship and injustice. With your large numbers, you are sending a message to the Islamic world that you have an unbreakable connection with al-Aqṣā Mosque." He continued to speak about the importance of this connection with al-Aqṣā and the injustice of occupation over the land of Isrā' and Mi'rāj.

He then mentioned the importance of the last ten days, during which the Prophet, peace be upon him, would increase his worship and devotion. He would perform i'tikāf in the last ten days each year, and twenty days in the final year of his life. 'Ā'ishah relates: "When the last ten nights would begin, the Messenger of God, peace be upon him, would keep awake at night, awaken his family and tighten his belt (prepare himself to be more diligent in worship)."[82] The Prophet used to offer night prayers until his feet would become swollen. When he was asked about that, he would say: "Shall I not be a grateful slave?"

Abū Hurayrah relates that the Prophet, peace be upon him, said: "God has angels that travel throughout the roads looking for those who remember God. Whenever they find people remembering God, they call out to them, saying, "Come to what you are looking for." Then the angels lower their wings around them until they cover up the lower sky. God asks them—though He knows better than they: "How did you find my servants?" The angels reply, "They glorify you, magnify you, praise you and exalt You."[83] God asks: "Do

---

[82] Ṣaḥīḥ Bukhārī: Kitāb faḍl laylat al-qadr—Bāb al-'amal fī al-'ashr al-awākhir min ramaḍān.

[83] These are exhibited through various formulations of the expressions—

they see me?" They reply, "No, O Lord." God says, "How would it be if they were to see Me?" The angels reply, "If they were to see You, they would worship You, exalt You, praise You, and glorify You even more devoutly and frequently." God says, "And what do they ask of Me?" The angels reply, "They ask You for Paradise." God says, "Did they see it?" The angels reply, "No." God says, "And how would they be were they to see it?" The angels reply, "Were they to see it, they would be even more eager and enthusiastic for it, with greater aspiration and desire." God asks, "From what do they seek refuge?" The angels reply, "They seek refuge from the Fire." God asks, "Did they see it?" The angels reply, "No." God asks, "And how it would it be had they seen it?" The angels reply, "Had they seen it, they would flee from it and hate it even more." Then God says, "My angels, I call you all to witness that I have forgiven them!" One of the angels says, "Lord, there is one among them that is not really one of them but happened to come for some other reason." God says, "They are still the same gathering, by virtue of whom their associates will not be made unfortunate."[84]

He then supplicated, "God, You are the Noble Pardoner who loves to pardon, so please pardon us;" along with other prayers.

He then mentioned the night of power and recited surah al-Qadr and the verse "*We revealed it on a Blessed Night, for We were intent on warning.*"[85] He mentioned that the Prophet, peace be upon him, would exert himself during the last ten days of Ramadan more than any other time of the year. He would perform iʿtikāf in the mosque during that time to seek out the Night of Power. He said, "Whoever spends the Night of Power in prayer out of faith and hope of reward, he will be forgiven his previous sins."[86] The imām then recited some supplications and sat down.

---

subḥānallāh, Allāhu akbar, and *al-ḥamdu lillāh,* among others.

[84] Ṣaḥīḥ Bukhārī: Kitāb al-daʿawāt—Bāb faḍl dhikrillāh.

[85] Qur'ān 44:3.

[86] Ṣaḥīḥ Bukhārī: Kitāb faḍl laylat al-qadr—Bāb al-ʿamal fī al-ʿashr al-awākhir min ramaḍān.

He then stood up at 1:10 pm for the second portion of the sermon and related the ḥadīth narrated by Ibn ʿUmar: God's Messenger, peace be upon him, enjoined the payment of one ṣāʿ[87] of dates or barley as zakat al-fiṭr on behalf of every Muslim, slave or free, male or female, young or old.[88] And he ordered that it be paid before the people went out to offer the Eid prayer. He also related the ḥadīth of Ibn ʿAbbās who narrated: The Messenger of God, peace be upon him, enjoined zakat al-fiṭr as a purification from any heedlessness and indecency, and a means of feeding the needy. It is accepted as zakāt for the person who pays it before the Eid prayer and as voluntary charity (ṣadaqah) for the person who pays it after the Eid prayer."[89] The imām encouraged its quick fulfillment because in our wealth, God has placed certain rights that belong to the needy. He then mentioned some Qurʾānic verses and ḥadīth reports encouraging charity, including: "*Take, [O, Muhammad], from their wealth a charity by which you purify them.*"[90]

Finally, he mentioned the fact that al-Aqṣā Mosque is under attack. He recited the verse: "*And who could be a greater wrongdoer than the one who forbids the mention of Allah's name in places of worship and strives for their ruin? Such people do not deserve to enter the places of worship, and, if they enter at all, they should do so in fear; for there is ignominy for them in this world and an awful punishment in the Hereafter.*"[91] He ended the Friday sermon with some final supplications.

We prayed Jumuʿah and returned to the hotel passing through demonstrations and protests organized by the Fatah and Hamas movements and arrived at the hotel at about 2:00 pm.

[87] Measure of volume that was roughly four hand-scoops, or 3 kg.

[88] Ṣaḥīḥ Bukhārī: Kitāb al-zakāt—Bāb ṣadaqat al-fiṭr ʿalā al-ṣaghīr wa al-kabīr.

[89] Related by Abū Dāwūd and Ibn Mājah, and authenticated by Ḥākim.

[90] Qurʾān 9:103.

[91] Qurʾān 2:114.

Ṣalāḥiyyah Khānqah

We left the hotel at 3:30 pm and arrived at the Dome of the Rock to meet other members of our group. We were to make our way to the Ṣalāḥiyyah Khānqah in order to pray 'Aṣr there. We exited to Bāb al-Silsilah and arrived at the Khanqah at 4:20 pm. After waiting for half an hour for the doors to open, we decided to leave and pray instead in the 'Umar Mosque.

Place of Khiḍr

We returned to al-Aqṣā entering from Bāb al-Silsilah at 5:15 pm and gathered at the Dome of the Rock near a canopy where it is said the Prophetic Ascension took place. Our attention was directed to an area attributed to Khiḍr. Here, I delivered a lecture on Khiḍr. In it, I mentioned the myths people invented about his lengthy life span. I mentioned the story of Ratan al-Hindī as recorded by Dhahabī:

> They claimed that he was a companion. 'Abd al-Wahhāb the noble Persian mystic and scholar said that he died around the year 632 AH. 'Abd al-Wahhāb had supposedly learned from Maḥmūd the son of Bābā Ratan, who was alive around 709 and had visited them in Shirāz. He mentioned that he was 176-years-old at the time, and was married with many children.
>
> As for whoever affirms these tall tales and believes in this long life span of Bābā Ratan, then we have no treatment for such a person. Know that I am the first to reject these, and that I am utterly incapable to debate such a person. It is not far-fetched that this was a Jinn who appeared in India who made these false claims, which people began to believe.
>
> This individual was a liar, deceiver and fabricator of the worse lies in order to collate a Pandora's box of uselessness and great disgrace. By the One Who people swear by, Ratan is surely a liar, may God destroy him. I have compiled a

> work of the fabricated narrators of this great deceiver which I entitled *Kasr wathan Ratan* ("Breaking the idol that is Ratan'). He was bold in his disobedience of God and claimed with little shame that he was a Companion, and 650 years old. He spread these lies among those who were unaware. I have exposed his falsehood in this work.[92]

I returned to the hotel around 6:00 pm. On the way, I met some people from our group who had lost their way and helped them with directions. As I walk through the streets of this land, I realize that the occupying state exists only by force and has no command over the hearts of people. On the way, people also asked me various jurisprudential questions, which I answered.

We broke our fasts in the hotel restaurant and left at 9:15 pm to pray 'Ishā' at the mosque. There was a massive crowd, and I could not find any place to pray except by the shoe racks near the entrance. The odor of the shoes was intense during prostration, as people inside and outside the mosque were pushing onto us. We remained patient, hoping for reward from God. In our spots, we prayed 'Ishā' and eight rak'ahs of Tarawīḥ. Most people here only pray eight rak'ahs of Tarawīḥ, after which they leave, leaving the mosque mostly empty and with only a handful of people to complete the rest of the rak'ahs of Tarawīḥ. I took this opportunity to proceed inside the mosque and complete the rest of my prayer.

[92] Pg. 517. Dhahabī. *Tārīkh al-islām wa wafayāt al-mashāhīr wa al-a'lām.*

LESSONS IN THE LAND OF IBRĀHĪM

7

LESSONS IN THE LAND OF IBRAHIM

Saturday 24th Ramadan 1436 AH

After the morning meal, Zayd reminded me that I would be teaching several classes today: the book *Patience of the Scholars* (*Ṣafaḥāt min ṣabr al-ʿulamāʾ*) before ʿAṣr, a class on Ghazālī's Iḥyāʾ ʿUlūm al-Dīn after ʿAṣr, and a general talk after Tarawīḥ followed by an exclusive session for sisters. I rested after Fajr and woke up at 10:00 am in order to recite some Qurʾān and review my lessons.

Saʿdī Neighbourhood

We exited the hotel at 11:30 am and entered the city from Bāb al-Sāhirah as usual. We visited a small mosque in the Saʿdī neighborhood called Shaykh Mikkī Mosque,[93] located in the old city of Jerusalem towards al-Aqṣā Mosque. Opposite to the Qādisiyyah School, the mosque was built to house the tomb of the pious scholar Shaykh Mikkī.[94] On the side is a building over which is written, 'Endowment of al-Ḥājj Naʿīm al-Khaṭīb al-Tamīmī Bū Saʿdī.'

Then we entered ʿAqaba Qādisiyyah Street with ʿAqaba Busṭāmī on our right and Mujāhidīn Road at the end.

---

[93] The origin of the mosque goes back to the 5th century AH/11th century CE.

[94] Abū al-Qāsim Mikkī b. ʿAbd al-Salām al-Rumaylī was an ʿAbbāsid-era Shāfiʿī muftī and ḥadīth scholar who lived in Jerusalem and was killed by invading Crusaders in 492/1099.

In al-Aqṣā Mosque

We entered the al-Aqṣā Mosque compound at 11:45 am, and to our left as we entered through King Faisal Gate were the gardens and Islamic schools of al-Aqṣā which were established in 1980.

The Dome of the Lovers of the Prophet

Facing the school to the south-east of King Faisal Gate is the dome of the Lovers of the Prophet ('Ushshāq al-Nabī'), which was built in 1233/1817 during the reign of Ottoman Sulṭān Maḥmūd II (d. 1839). It is currently named so because it hosts certain Sufi gatherings in its premise. It is open on all sides, rectangular, built on four pillars, and contains a niche of beautiful hollow stone. There are three steps that lead into the platform from the western and eastern sides.

Department of Women's Affairs

In front of the dome is the Department of Women's Affairs in a building with a small dome with many surrounding olive trees. It is called the Dome of Sulaymān referring to the Umayyad Caliph Sulaymān b. 'Abd al-Mālik (d. 99/717). The current building dates to the Ayyūbid era, being constructed in 600/1203 and renovated in the Ottoman era.

Bāb al-Ghawānimah

Then we entered the Ghawānimah Gate, one of the doors of al-Aqṣā Mosque, located in the north-west. It was constructed by al-Walīd son of 'Abd al-Malik b. Marwān (d. 96/715).

Bāb al-Nāẓir

We left for Bāb al-Nāẓir (Inspector's Gate), also known as Bāb al-Majlis (Council Gate), as it is situated next to the Islamic Scholars Council. This gate exists to the west of the mosque and was first built in the Umayyad period and later expanded in the Mamlūk period. Outside the gate is Buṣīrī Road, which was constructed in

839/1436 during the reign of the Mamlūk Sulṭān Ashraf Sayf al-Dīn Barsbay (d. 841/1438), or possibly even earlier than that. There is another path next to it which was constructed in 613 AH.

Bab al-Ḥadīd

We passed through Bāb al-Ḥadīd (Iron Gate) which is in the western gallery between the Bāb al-Nāẓir and Bab al-Qaṭṭānīn (Cotton Merchant Gate). Close to it is the tomb of King Ḥusayn b. ʿAlī (d. 1350/1931) who was the father of the King of Jordan Abdullah I (d. 1370/1951).

Bab al-Qaṭṭānīn

We visited Bāb al-Qaṭṭānīn, one of the most beautiful and largest gates of the al-Aqṣā Mosque, located in the middle of its western wall between Bāb al-Ḥadīd to the north and Bab al-Maṭharah (Ablution Gate) to the south. It leads to the cotton market, which is one of the oldest remaining Jerusalem markets. The Mamlūk Prince Tankaz al-Nāṣirī (d. 741/1340) refurbished this door in 737/1336 during the reign of Mamlūk Sulṭān Muḥammad b. Qalāwūn (d. 742/1341). It was renovated again by the Supreme Islamic Council in 1929. At the door lies the tomb of Aḥmad Ḥilmī ʿAbd al-Bāqī (d. 1963),[95] which has a path in front of it.

The Tomb of Muḥammad ʿAlī Jawhar

To the side lies another tomb, this one belonging to the great mujāhid and Indian leader Maulānā Muḥammad ʿAlī. He died in London on the 15th of Shaʿbān and was buried in Jerusalem on Friday 5th Ramadan in 1349/1931. The door of his tomb bears the following: '*Their Lord gives them good news of mercy from Himself and His good pleasure and gardens, wherein lasting blessings shall be theirs.*'[96]

---

[95] Known as Aḥmad Ḥilmī Pasha, he was a soldier, economist, and politician, who served in various post-Ottoman Empire governments, and was Prime Minister of the short-lived All-Palestine Government in the Gaza Strip.
[96] Qur'ān 9:21.

Muḥammad ʿAlī Jawhar was one of India's top political leaders, known for his endless support of Muslims and defense of the Ottoman caliphate in international assemblies. In 1919, he formed the famous Khilafat Movement along with his brother in order to support the dying Ottoman Caliphate. He withdrew from the Indian National Congress Party after they rejected certain demands of Indian Muslims. He passed away on the 4th of January 1931 in London while attending a political conference. His body was transported to Jerusalem, where a royal procession took place before he was buried in al-Aqṣā Mosque precincts in accordance with his will and in recognition of his services to support Palestine and defend its holy sites by the Muftī of Jerusalem.

Madrasah Asharafiyyah

Between Bāb al-Qaṭṭānīn and Bāb al-Silsilah lies the Ashrafiyyah School which was built in 876 AH by Mamlūk Sulṭān al-Ashraf Abū al-Naṣr Qaitbay (d. 901/1496). The school has two sections: one inside and one outside al-Aqṣā Mosque. The inner one is comprised of two floors: the first is the prayer space for the Ḥanbalīs.[97] A portion is currently used as a center for the Manuscript Section of the al-Aqṣā Mosque Library, while a larger part houses the al-Aqṣā Secondary School for Girls, founded in 1998. Within it is also the tomb of Shaykh Muḥammad b. Muḥammad al-Khalīlī (d. 1147/1734),[98] and some residential units.

The roof of the school's mosque on the second floor was destroyed due to the destruction of the earthquake of 1346/1927. Somewhere on the surviving walls are the following words inscribed with beautiful Mamlūk inscriptions in large letters: 'This Ashrafiyyah School was founded by Maulānā Sulṭān King al-Ashraf Abū al-Naṣr

[97] One of the four Sunnī schools of jurisprudence.

[98] He was a renowned Azhar-educated Shāfiʿī scholar and jurist, native of Hebron, who lived in Jerusalem as its Muftī. A lover and collector of books, he endowed his massive personal library of books and manuscripts to the public.

Qaitbay at the beginning of the month of Rabīʿ al-Awwal in the year 875. This was in the days of Maulānā al-Muʿizz al-Nāṣirī Sīdī Muḥammad al-Khāzandār, Custodian of the Two Holy Mosque, may God magnify his state.'

The Dome of Yūsuf

In front of the Dome of the Rock towards the qiblah lies a small dome called the Dome of Yūsuf. On it is written the following: 'In the name of God, the Most Gracious, the Most Merciful. May His blessing be upon Muḥammad the Prophet and his family. The construction of this building and the digging of its foundation was ordered by our Master King Sulṭān Ṣalāh al-Dīn, Sulṭān of Islam and Muslims, Custodian of the Two Holy Mosques and this al-Aqṣā mosque Abū al-Muẓaffar Yūsuf b. Ayyūb, Reviver of the State, Commander of the Faithful—may God lengthen his days and support his banner—during the time of the great leader Sayf al-Dīn ʿAlī b. Aḥmad in the year 585 AH.'

This is perhaps the first historical evidence of the use of the title 'Custodian of the Two Holy Mosques.'

Ẓuhr prayer in the Qiblī Mosque

Next, I went to the Qiblī Mosque and moved to the front near the position of the imām. The adhān was called after which I prayed two rakʿahs of sunnah prayer. The time between the adhān and the prayer was quite lengthy. The Imām came and stressed to everyone that the one who can pray standing should not pray sitting on the chairs as this will invalidate his prayers. The prayers started a little after 1:00 pm. As I was leaving after the prayers, I was surprised to hear another iqāmah[99] being called for prayer. I then remembered that they combine the ʿAṣr with Ẓuhr prayers for travelers, who

[99] This is the second call to prayer which is sounded within the prayer space to signal the start of the prayer.

usually happen to be in large numbers. However, the designated Imām would also lead ʿAṣr prayer later at its normal time.

I arrived at the hotel about 1:30 pm, rested a little, and woke up after one hour to prepare for my classes.

Lecture on Patience of the Scholars (Ṣafaḥāt min ṣabr al-ʿulamāʾ)

I began the lesson at 3:30 pm by first reminding the audience of the need to seek knowledge through intensive and deep study by acquiring it from the people of knowledge who are experts in their fields and engaged in teaching. They should not seek knowledge from preachers or speakers, since each field has its experts.

I also explained that education in Islam involves training people to become wise persons, whereas education in secular institutions is designed to promote skills and expertise in order to help students earn money and wealth.

I explained the verse, "*You will find me, if God wills, of the patient ones.*"[100] I explained the proper use of the expressions 'inshāʾAllāh,' 'mashāʾAllāh,' 'al-ḥamdu lillāh,' 'tabārakallāh,' and 'subḥānallāh.' Finally, I removed what I saw as some misconceptions about faith in the unseen.

Lesson from Iḥyāʾ ʿUlūm al-Dīn

I began the lesson on Iḥyāʾ ʿUlūm al-Dīn at 5:30 pm in the Marwānī prayer hall by summarizing the meaning of the Qurʾānic term 'ḥanīfiyyah' and the significance of the leadership of Ibrāhīm. I stressed that there should be no object in the mosque that would attract the attention of the worshiper, for the mosque is the place where ḥanīfiyyah is developed. I also explained that God created the world full of pleasures, and that these are not necessarily forbidden, so long as a person doesn't engross himself within them thereby forgetting God. Rather, he must always be focused on God

---

[100] Qurʾān 37:102.

and indifferent towards everything and everyone else. Everything in the world has been created for human beings, and human beings have been created to worship God alone.

I warned them, and myself, of death, as there was to be a funeral prayer in the mosque after 'Aṣr prayer. I informed them that this funeral is a great reminder. I taught them how to perform the funeral prayer, and that there are four takbīrāt[101] according to Abū Ḥanīfah and most Imāms. I taught them what is to be recited between these takbīrāt.

I then read to them from the Iḥyā' some of the statements of the Followers concerning death, which included the following:

Upon approaching death, the caliph 'Umar b. 'Abd al-'Azīz asked some scholars for advice. They said: "You are not the first caliph who will pass away." He asked for more. They replied, "There isn't a single one of your forefathers, all the way until Adam, who has not tasted death, and now it is your turn." 'Umar began to weep.

It is said that Rabī' b. Khaytham was known to have dug a grave in his house and to sleep in it for some time every day in order to strengthen the remembrance of death. He used to say: "If the remembrance of death parts from me even for a moment I would be destroyed."

Muṭarrif b. 'Abdullah b. Shikhkhīr said, "This death has taken away comfort from the rich, so ask God for the comfort that is everlasting."

'Umar b. 'Abd al-'Azīz advised 'Anbasah: "Remember death as much as you can because if you are living in comfort, that will take it away; but if you are living in constrained circumstances, then it will be an opening for you."

---

[101] Takbīr (plural, takbīrāt) is the practice of saying 'Allāhu akbar' aloud during prayer, usually to signal the beginning and shifting from one stage to another of prayer.

Abū Sulaymān al-Dārānī said: I said to Umm Hārūn: Do you love death? She replied: No. I asked: Why not? She replied: "If I was disobedient to a man, I would not want to meet him, so how would I want to meet God when I have disobeyed Him?"

In the end, I answered questions, including how supplication can benefit the deceased when it is not from one's own actions, and whether it was permissible to pray for one's non-Muslim relatives.

A Lecture after Tarawīḥ Prayers

In my lecture after Tarawīḥ prayers, I focused on the importance of prayer (ṣalāh) in general and stressed that the prayers should be performed in congregation in mosques because of the immense reward in that and the dire warnings against not doing so. I also spoke about the extra reward of prayer in the three Holy Mosques. As for the optional prayers, then it is better to pray them at home and without congregation. I mentioned the Prophetic practice in that, along with the sayings of various scholars.

Women's Session

At 12:00 am midnight there was an exclusive women's session where I answered various questions on knowledge, finding an experienced and sincere teacher, traveling for the sake of knowledge, and the issue of women traveling alone. There were also questions pertaining to Sufism, Sufi orders, following a specific jurisprudential school versus choosing between them, and wiping over socks during ablution. Some of them approached me and thanked me by saying: "We appreciate the fact that you have made the matters of religion easier for us, and hence more endearing." I replied: "Religion is meant to be easy, and God only wants from us what benefits us, for He is the most Merciful of merciful ones."

TRAVELS FROM WEST TO EAST

8

TRAVELS FROM WEST TO EAST

Sunday 25th Ramadan 1436 AH

After our customary suḥūr meal, Fajr prayer, and morning rest, I went out with my family at 11:30 am to see al-Aqṣā Mosque and its facilities.

The Tomb of al-Budayrī

We entered al-Aqṣā from Bāb al-Ḥiṭṭah and turned to the arena in front of Bāb al-Nāẓir. We visited the grave of the eminent scholar Shaykh Muḥammad b. Budayr b. Muḥammad b. Maḥmūd b. Ḥubaysh al-Shāfiʿī al-Maqdisī from the Budayrī family, who died in 1220 AH.

Noted chronicler Jabartī in *Ajāʾib al-Āthār fī Tarājim wa al-Akhbār* states that Shaykh Muḥammad b. Budayr came to Egypt with his father around 1160 AH. There, he learned the Qurʾān and other disciplines, and first attended the lessons of Shaykh ʿĪsā al-Barāwī. He then turned his sights to new disciplines by studying with Shaykh ʿAṭiyyah al-Ajhūrī, staying with him until his death. He then heard Ṣaḥīḥ Muslim from Shaykh Aḥmad al-Rāshidī and then spent time with our Shaykh Maḥmūd al-Kurdī. He withdrew himself from people but they only honored him even more. Shaykh al-Kurdī sent him to Jerusalem, where he took up residence in al-Aqṣā and began to teach people various sciences and conduct circles of dhikr. He had a good understanding of matters and a sharp mind. He had a good standing with people and was well loved by all, even leaders and ministers, to the point that his intercession was highly valued. In 1182, he wrote to our Shaykh Murtaḍā to seek ijāzah and received the response in a treatise entitled *Qalansuwah al-Tāj*. He continued to teach, remind, and illuminate others until his passing in the year 1220. He left a void that no one could fill.

Al-Burrāq Mosque

We visited a dome in front of Bāb al-Silsilah upon which is written 'Dār al-Qur'ān al-Karīm.' A few steps over is a sign for al-Burrāq Mosque, which is close to the now closed Moroccan Gate dating back to the Umayyad period. We walked to the mosque and stayed inside for a short time.

Museum of Islamic Antiquities

We entered the Museum of Islamic Antiquities which was built by the Supreme Islamic Council in 1923 with the aim of preserving Islamic monuments in Jerusalem. It includes a large selection of historical artifacts, art and other items, as well as many remnants of ancient buildings and decorations.

We saw the remains of the pulpit of the al-Aqṣā Mosque, which was burned by an Australian-natural extremist named Denis Michael Rohan in 1969. This pulpit was constructed in Damascus in 1168 CE in the time of Nūr al-Dīn Zengī. Sulṭān Ṣalāh al-Dīn ordered it to be brought to Jerusalem after its liberation from the Crusaders in 1180.

Wooden ornamental vaults can be seen inside the pulpit of Ṣalāh al-Dīn and date back to the Ottoman period. The head of the pulpit is made from wood and decorated with colorful floral motifs that are red, yellow and green, also dating back to the Ottoman period. The pulpit used to be prominently visible in al-Aqṣā Mosque. There are also four Ottoman-era engravings by calligrapher Ḥusām al-Dīn Khoqandī compiled in 1292 AH which used to be seen above the doors of the Dome of the Rock from the inside.

The museum also houses pottery jars dating back to various Islamic periods which were used to store water and oil, and firearms from the Ottoman period. We also saw coins and golden dinars from several Islamic periods.

There was a lamp which was used for lighting inside the al-Aqṣā Mosque prior to the use of electricity in 1931. The al-Aqṣā Mosque used to be lit by 10,000 lamps powered by oil which was extracted from an oil well located at the bottom of the Grammar Dome (al-Qubbah al-Naḥawiyyah) near Bāb al-Silsilah. The lamp was gifted by the Mamlūk Emir of Damascus Tankaz for his school in Jerusalem, the Tankazī School. This was later transferred to the Ibrāhīmī Mosque in Hebron, and in 1927, to the museum. It is adorned with the Qur'ānic verse: "*The mosques of God are only maintained by those who believe in God and the Last Day.*"[102]

There were also uniforms worn by Shaykh Muḥammad al-Khalīlī,[103] Mufti of Jerusalem and Hebron from the Ottoman period. These include a cloak, two head coverings and a metal symbol containing God's name which used to adorn the green flag that was carried on official occasions.

Al-Aqṣā Mosque Library

Next to the museum is the library of al-Aqṣā Mosque, whose building was formerly known as the 'Women's Mosque.' The library was first opened in 1922 and now contains 4,000 manuscripts, including a large number of copies of the Qur'ān, a number of manuscripts in Ottoman Turkish, and thousands of books and magazines both old and new. It is estimated that there are more than 160,000 books on various subjects.

---

[102] Qur'ān 9:18.

[103] See footnote 98.

Ẓuhr Prayer

I prayed Ẓuhr in the mosque and met a Palestinian intellectual who had completed a doctorate in Britain. We spoke in English. Afterwards, I went back to the hotel to rest for a while.

Lecture from the Patience of the Scholars (Ṣafaḥāt min Ṣabr al-'Ulamā')

I went down to the lecture hall at 3:00 pm to teach from *Ṣafaḥāt min Ṣabr al-'Ulamā'*. Today I referenced the story of Baqīyy b. Makhlad. 'Abd al-Raḥmān b. Aḥmad b. Baqīyy b. Makhlad relates: I heard my father relate that his father (Imām Baqīyy b. Makhlad) traveled from Makkah to Baghdad for the purpose of meeting Imām Aḥmad b. Ḥanbal. Baqīyy stated:

When I approached Baghdad, news reached me of the inquisition of Imām Aḥmad and his being banned from public contact. I was overtaken by grief. Nevertheless, I entered the city of Baghdad and rented a room at an inn. I then came to the main mosque to sit with people. I came to a great gathering wherein someone was speaking about ḥadīth narrators. I was told that this was Yaḥyā b. Ma'īn. I made my way closer to him and asked: "O Abu Zakariyya, may God have mercy on you! I am a traveler far from home who wishes to ask you a question so please do not refuse me." He replied: "Go ahead." I asked him about a number of narrators I had come across, to each of which he responded appropriately, praising some and critiquing others. I asked him about Hishām b. 'Ammār, to which he replied: "His name was Abū al-Walīd, and he led prayers in Damascus. He was reliable, in fact, more than reliable. Had he harbored any bit of arrogance, it would have not diminished his high standing because of his goodness and virtue." The other participants in the audience shouted to me, "That's enough, God have mercy on you! Others also have questions!" While standing on my feet, I said: "Tell me about one more person: Aḥmad b. Ḥanbal." He looked at me with amazement before saying: "Can a person like me be asked about

Imam Aḥmad?! Verily that is the leader of all the Muslims and the best and most exalted of them."

I then went out in search of the house of Imām Aḥmad. I finally found it and knocked on the door. When he came out, I said to him: "O Abū 'Abdullah! I am a stranger far away from his home and this is my first time in this town. I am a student of Hadith who is collecting the Sunnah and I have not undertaken this journey except to benefit from you."

He said to me, "Come to this passage and make sure no one lays their eyes on you." I entered that place and he asked me, "Where are you from?" I replied: "From the far west." He asked, "From Africa?" I replied: "Farther than that, for I have to cross the sea to go to Africa. I am from Andalus." He said, "Your land is very far indeed. Nothing is more beloved to me than to assist a person like you, but I have been afflicted in ways perhaps you may have heard of." I said, "Of course, I heard of it, but O Abu 'Abdullah! This is the first time I have come here. No one knows who I am, so if you permit, I will come every day in the clothes of a beggar and call out at the door as they normally do. Then you could come to this passage and if you only narrate to me one ḥadīth a day it would be sufficient for me." He replied, "Yes, on condition that you do not show yourself to anyone, not even the scholars of ḥadīth." I replied, "I accept your conditions."

I would thus take a stick in my hand, wrap a stained cloth on my head and come to his door and call out in the manner of the local beggars: "Reward! God have mercy on you!" Then he would come to the passage and narrate to me two or three ḥadīth—and sometimes even more. I maintained this practice until the ruler responsible for the inquisition died and was succeeded by one who was a follower of the sunnah. It was then that Imām Aḥmad became visible again and attained prominence as an Imām and people began to flock to him. Yet, Imām Aḥmad recognized my persistence and whenever I came to his circles, he would make room for me and would tell my story to the others. He would present ḥadīth to me, sometimes reading them to me and sometimes listening to my reading.

Once I fell ill and was forced to undergo treatment, which made me miss his sessions. I sent him word of my illness upon which he immediately set forth to visit me along with some other people that were with him. There I was, lying down in my rented room and wrapped in my cloak, with my books at my head, when I heard a commotion at the inn. I heard people saying: "It's him! Look! The Imām of the Muslims is coming!" The innkeeper rushed to me, saying, "O Abū 'Abd al-Raḥmān, the Imām of the Muslims, Abū 'Abdullah Aḥmad b. Ḥanbal has come to visit you!" Imām Aḥmad came in my room and sat by my bedside. His companions crowded the room, and some of them had to stand, with their pens in their hands. Imām Aḥmad prayed for me sufficing with the following words, which were inscribed by those around me: "Abū 'Abd al-Raḥmān, rejoice in God's reward! We often enjoy good health with no tinge of sickness, or illness with no hope for good health, May God raise you to good health and bless you with His healing power."

Imām Aḥmad soon departed, and the residents of the inn came and started to treat me gently. In fact, their caring for me was greater than I would have received had I been among my own family, all because of the visit of a righteous man.

Lesson from Iḥyā' 'Ulūm al-Dīn

We prayed 'Aṣr in the mosque and went to the Marwānī prayer area to sit and listen to the Qur'ānic recitation until 5:30 pm. I then started the lesson and explained to them the meaning of ḥanīfiyyah, īmān and Islam in light of the story of Ibrāhīm. I then answered their questions, including a question of whether the Qur'ān has referred to our religion as Islam, and whether Islam exists before īmān.

Breakfast with the Director of al-Aqṣā Mosque

We went back to the hotel and broke our fast with Shaykh ʿOmar al-Kiswānī, director of al-Aqṣā Mosque. He was known for his noble and courageous stance on the Palestine issue and defense of Islamic sites. He spoke to us about the critical conditions being experienced by Palestinian Muslims. He talked about al-Quds University, which is not recognized by the Israeli state. He also spoke about the Imāms of al-Aqṣā and the reason for their being two congregations: one in the Dome of the Rock and one in the Qiblī Mosque.

A Short Talk on Supplication

We prayed ʿIshāʾ and Tarawīḥ prayers in the Qiblī Mosque, and then I went up to the Dome of the Rock to give a lesson on worship, duʿāʾ (supplication) and the true meaning of supplication. I explained why the answer from God is sometimes delayed and I stressed the great reward in supplication as it is the essence of worship. I mentioned that when God delays the granting of a supplication, it is never because He is incapable or miserly, but rather, it is always for the greater interests of the worshipers, so we should never fall behind in the matter of worship and supplication.

Answering Questions

We went back to the hotel and I sat with the male members of the group to answer various questions, which included combining between prayers while traveling, the traveling of females without a guardian, praying voluntary prayers in congregation, traveling for knowledge, the real reason for the state of women in Muslim societies, taking knowledge from its primary sources, zakāt charity, its recipients, and its proper distribution between relatives, neighbors and the poor in other countries.

BLESSED NIGHT

9

BLESSED NIGHT

Monday 26th Ramadan 1436 AH

After having our morning meal and praying Fajr, we awoke again at 9:00 am in order to visit the museum and another library.

Museum of Islamic Antiquities

We visited the museum again around 11:30 am. Today, we saw two astrolabes, one of them from the 18th century, used for astronomical calculations and determining direction. We also saw an Ottoman-era wooden sundial for measuring distances and time, a scissor for wax-cutting, an inkpot, and a device for working on precious stones and jewels.

This museum contains many manuscripts and rare documents, including a total of 266 Qur'ānic manuscripts and about 1,000 Mamlūk documents relating to a variety of social and economic affairs. We examined the second half of a Qur'ānic manuscript in Easter Kufic unvowelled script, with fifteen lines per page and the names of the chapters written in golden rectangular ribbons in Kufic script. The style and size of each line varied, in the manner of antique Islamic designs. At the end of the manuscript, it was indicated that this was written by Ḥasan b. Ḥusayn b. 'Alī b. Abū Ṭālib. This manuscript was gifted to the Dome of the Rock and is considered the oldest Qur'ānic manuscript in the museum.

We also saw a very large Mamlūk-era Qur'ānic copy dating to the 15th century CE. The first half was written in muḥaqqiq Qur'ānic script. It ranks second in terms of size at the museum. It was apparently written by more than one calligrapher, and the first 56 pages have been replaced by a more modern script.

We saw another Mamlūk Qur'ānic manuscript which was gifted by Sulṭān Ashraf Barsbay (d. 841/1438) and brought to al-Aqṣā Mosque in 1432. It is the largest Qur'ān in the museum, being 107 cm long, 90 cm wide and 15 cm thick.

We examined a smaller-sized Qur'ān that was gifted by Enver Pasha, an Ottoman military officer, in 1916. This Qur'ān is a great model of calligraphy as it was written by the famous calligrapher 'Uthmān b. Ḥusayn, more famously known as Kāishzādeh. It was ornamented in gold by his student Ḥājj Aḥmad and the names of the chapters written by Muḥammad 'Alī Baktāiji 'Alī Pasha.

There was also a very beautiful Ottoman-script Qur'ān gifted by Prince Bayezid, son of Sulaymān the Magnificent. Later on, additional texts were added describing Bayezid as a Sulṭān after a failed revolution against his father which resulted in the prince's own death. It was gifted by Fāṭimah bint Nīrafur on behalf of the deceased Ya'qūb Pasha and his wife, and supervised by Shaykh Muḥammad al-Danaf. It was written by Muḥammad Laṭīf in Naskh script.

There was also a copy of the Qur'ān, of which only twelve parts remain, which was donated by Oghl Khātūn, the daughter of Prince Muḥammad the son of prince Tamaq. She gifted it to the female zāwiyah which was built to the west of the al-Aqṣā compound.

There was also a Qur'ānic copy of Sulṭān Abū al-Ḥasan al-Marīnī, ruler of Morocco, dating to 1331 CE written in beautiful Moroccan script which was gifted to the al-Aqṣā Mosque. It was brought from Morocco in a chest ornamented by silver and engraved strips.

The museum also contained an oiled wooden chest containing a complete manuscript of the Qur'ān in thirty parts written on paper and gifted by Sulṭān Murad III (1574-1595 CE) son of Sulṭān Selīm II.

It also contains the first half of a Qur'ān gifted to al-Aqṣā Mosque and completed in 1705 by order of the governor of Jerusalem Mustafa Pasha under the supervision of the Grand Mufti of Jerusalem Shaykh Muḥammad al-Khalīlī.[104] It contains a Persian translation of the verses between the lines.

Al-Aqṣā Mosque Library

We also visited the library of al-Aqṣā Mosque next to the museum, where I met Shaykh Yūsuf al-Uzbekī who is the director of manuscripts. He is a great scholar and specialist who has done extensive work on manuscripts, many of which have been published by Dār al-Bashāir al-Islāmiyyah. He is close to our companions Shaykh Nāẓim Ya'qūbī, Shaykh 'Abdullah Ṭūm and others. He is courteous, humble, and gentle in his speech. He is currently devoted to completing a work on ḥadīth narration in Jerusalem.

He gifted me some of his own works and those of Dr. Ḥusām al-Dīn Mūsā 'Affānah. He informed me that Dr. Ḥusām al-Dīn is the most knowledgeable scholar in Palestine but is forbidden from entering Jerusalem. He promised me that he would try to arrange a meeting for me. He gave me the catalogue of manuscripts stored in the library so I could choose which ones I would like to have copies of. He also referred me to some libraries at Bāb al-Nāẓir where I could buy the books I needed.

I prayed the Ẓuhr and 'Aṣr prayers in al-Aqṣā Mosque and returned to the hotel to rest for a bit.

Lessons from the Patience of the Scholars (Ṣafaḥāt min Ṣabr al-'Ulamā')

At 3:00 pm I arose to teach our lessons from *Ṣafaḥāt min Ṣabr al-'Ulamā'*. Today I shared the incredible journey of Abū Hatim al-Rāzī which is narrated by his son who heard his father say:

---

[104] See footnote 98.

The very first journey I ever undertook to learn ḥadīth lasted for seven years. I counted my steps as comprising a total distance of 1,000 leagues.[105] In fact, I continued to count until I reached 1,000 and then I stopped. I could not recall how many times I walked from Kūfah to Baghdad, or from Makkah to Madīnah. I once left Bahrayn near the city of Ṣilā and walked all the way to Egypt, and from Egypt to Ramlah, Ramlah to Jerusalem, Ramlah to Aschelon, Ramlah to Tiberias, Tiberias to Damascus, Damascus to Homs, Homs to Antakya, and Antakya to Tarsus.[106] I returned from Tarsus to Homs because there were some ḥadīth of Abū al-Yamān remaining to be heard. I then left Homs for Baysān,[107] and from there to al-Raqqah, and from there I traveled on the Euphrates to Baghdad. There I traveled from Wāsiṭ to Nīl[108] and from there to Kūfah. All of these travels were on foot and on my first journey, when I was twenty years old. I had traveled for a total of seven years.

I left Ray in the year 213 AH. I arrived in Kūfah in Ramadan while the ʿAbdullah b. Yazīd the Qurʾānic scholar was still alive in Makkah. We received the news of his passing while we were in Kūfah. I returned in the year 221. I went on another journey that lasted three years in the year 242 and returned in 245. I went to Tarsus in 217 or 218, when its governor was Ḥasan b. Muṣʿab. I was looking at him as if he were a ḥadīth scholar. He was red-headed, wearing a cap and shawl. I presumed that he looked like Sinīd b. Dāwūd.

---

[105] A farsakh is a unit of distance used throughout the ancient Near-East that is based on paces of walking. Estimates vary based on geographical regions, but the modern farsakh has been fixed at 10 km, whereas in premodern times it was closer to 5. So, 1,000 farsakh=5,000 km=3000 miles.
[106] Historic city in south-central Turkey.
[107] Beit She'an in northern Palestine.
[108] Northeast of Baghdad.

Perhaps I had seen the governor and presumed him to be Sinīd, or perhaps they were together and I mixed the two.

I also mentioned the case of Khalīl b. Aḥmad al-Farāhīdī. His student Naḍr b. Shumayl says, "Khalīl was living in a simple hut in Baṣrah and did not own even two coins, while his companions used their knowledge to acquire wealth. Khalīl used to receive a pension from Sulaymān b. Habib b. al-Muhallab b. Abī Ṣufrah al-Azdī, the governor of Persia and Ahwāz. Once the governor sent him a request to come teach his children personally, but Khalīl declined and wrote back the following verses:

The governor should know that I am fine.
Great affluence is mine without the wealth.
I covet only my own self
Because I've seen none die of famished health.

For sure, provision stands as fixed
Waning not for weaker ones
It never does intensify
For powerful and mighty ones.

In turn, the governor canceled his stipend, and Khalīl responded with another verse:

He who shaped my mouth will feed it
so long as life in me remains
You did suppress me from a little good
But that for you will reap no gains.[109]

Embarrassed, the governor responded with a letter apologizing and increasing his stipend.

I also summarized the story of Abū ʿAlī al-Qālī of Baghdad. Abū Naṣr Hārūn b. Mūsā relates that he used to attend the dictation

[109] See pg. 1267, Yāqūt al-Ḥamawī, *Muʿjam al-Udabāʾ*.

circles of Abū ʿAlī in Zahrā school in Córdoba during the spring season. Once while walking to the lesson, it began to rain and he arrived soaking wet. Abū ʿAlī, surrounded by notables of Córdoba, asked me to come closer, saying, "Take it easy Abū Naṣr, and don't worry about what happened to you, for that is something that will go away from you as quickly as you change your clothes." He then said, "My body has been afflicted with permanent scars which will remain until my grave!" He explained:

"I used to attend the circles of Ibn Mujāhid. I once set out at night to get to his circle. When I arrived at the end of the path that led to his teaching place, I found it closed with a gate that was difficult to open. I thought to myself, 'Glory be to God, I came so early to get a good spot, but it is looking difficult!' I looked around and found a tunnel. I entered it in order to get through. About mid-way, I got stuck and could neither back out nor go forward. I somehow managed to force myself through but only after ripping my clothes and parts of my body which caused a fracture in one of my bones. But God graced me to come out and attend the circles in this state!" He then recited some poetry.

Abū Naṣr said: We wrote this down before we got to the lesson. He made me forget my own ordeal, which was insignificant compared to his. After this, I began to attend his lessons even more, and did not leave him until he passed away, God have mercy on him.

Lesson from Iḥyāʾ ʿUlūm al-Dīn

After ʿAṣr prayers, I continued our lessons from Iḥyāʾ ʿUlūm al-Dīn, this time focusing on the sections on death and decreasing aspirations.

The Messenger of God, peace be upon him, said to ʿAbdullah b. ʿUmar, "When you wake up in the morning, then do not concern yourself with the evening. And when you reach the evening, do not concern yourself with the morning. Take from your health before illness strikes, and from your life before your death. Indeed, O slave of God! You do not know what your description shall be tomorrow."[110]

'Alī narrated that the Prophet, peace be upon him, said, "The worst that I fear for you are two qualities: following desires and excessive aspirations. Following desires takes you away from the truth, while excessive aspirations represent love for this world." He also said, "God grants the world to those whom He loves as well as those He hates. When He loves a servant, He grants him faith. Know that the religion has its children, while the world also has its children. So be the children of religion not the world. Know that this world is leaving away while the next life is coming ahead. Know that today is a day of action and no account, and you are headed for a day of account and no action."[111]

I concluded the lesson quickly. I felt great pain in my eyes and went back to the hotel to rest.

The Twenty-Seventh Night

After breaking our fast in the hotel and resting for a bit, we went out around 9:15 pm to the mosque. We found a busy road, full of congregants seeking to stay awake on this blessed night. The crowds were immense by every measure, and far greater than the congregants that had attended the Friday prayers. When we approached Bāb al-Ḥiṭṭah, we saw people returning back as it was closed because of the over-crowding. There was no further place in the mosque from that entrance. We ultimately entered the mosque from the Ghawānimah Gate, along with a slow-moving, tightly-packed throng of people. We feared that the door would be closed making us miss our prayers. When we finally found ourselves within the mosque, we praised God, and our anguish was relieved. I saw a space in a passage between some people next to the terrace

[110] Tirmidhī: Kitāb al-zuhd—Bāb mā jā'a fī qaṣr al-amal.

[111] This is listed as a weak narration in 'Alī al-Ḥalabī's *Mausū'ah al-āḥādīth wa al-āthār al-da'īfah wa al-mauḍū'ah.*

in front of the Bāb al-Qaṭṭānīn, which I quickly occupied. From there, I performed 'Ishā', Tarawīḥ and Witr prayers.

The Imām prolonged the Qunūt supplication[112] to an extent that I have never witnessed in my entire life. When I finished my prayer, I headed to the Dome of the Rock where I was scheduled to teach a class. I had to pass through great crowds and weave through rows of men and women. When I arrived there, I found out that the class had been rearranged. I returned back to the hotel in a slow journey that took far longer than usual.

Meeting with the Women

There was another appointed meeting with the women in our group to answer their questions, which included questions on women's covering (ḥijāb, niqāb), women's prayer on the outside, the prayer of women while men may be looking at them, and other questions related to their affairs.

[112] See footnote 26.

SERMON ON THE MOUNT OF OLIVES

10

SERMON ON THE MOUNT OF OLIVES

Tuesday 27th Ramadan 1436 AH

In the morning, we visited some markets inside the walls of the old city in order to buy clothes and gifts. Located on the sides of smaller streets, these shops resemble ancient markets established by the Ayyūbid, Mamlūk and Ottoman civilizations in various cities such as Damascus and Cairo, which are well-known for their architectural beauty and their alluring buildings and domes.

Zāwiyah Naqshabandī Mosque

At 11:30 am, we visited the Zāwiyah Naqshabandī Mosque near the Ghawānimah Gate. Also known as the Uzbek, or Bukhārī, Zāwiyah as an attribution to its founders, it was established in the late Mamlūk or early Ottoman era. The Sufi Shaykh Usman Beg of Bukhārā expanded it in 1731 in a wonderful and masterful construction. We entered through its main gate into a small narrow corridor that led to its small mosque, and then to a burial chamber that housed the graves of several Naqshbandī scholars. We then climbed some stairs that led to a portion developed by the Ottomans into a scholarly library.

Bāb Qaṭṭānīn Market

We strolled around Bāb Qaṭṭānīn Market where I purchased some clothes for my daughters and gifts for their children. We entered a shop owned by a respectable man named Muḥammad al-Rajabī, a member of the Zakat Committee of Jerusalem and head of a charity that sponsors orphans. He has travelled to Britain repeatedly and currently is running a campaign to encourage Muslims from all over the world to visit Jerusalem.

The Bāb Qaṭṭānīn Market is one of the oldest markets in Jerusalem. It was established by the Mamlūk Prince Tankaz al-Nāṣirī and refurbished by Sulṭān al-Nāṣir Muḥammad ibn Qalāwūn in 727 AH. In the Mamlūk period, it was considered the finest, busiest and most beautiful market in the city.

Cotton and silk cloth from India is sold in the market. In the middle is a men's bath known as Ḥammām al-Shifā and in front of it, to the west, is a road that leads to an Islamic orphanage.

We combined Ẓuhr and ʿAṣr prayer in a gallery between Bāb al-Nāẓir and Bāb al-Muṭahhirah, and then visited local bookshops to buy some books. We finally returned to our hotels exhausted and eagerly went to bed to rest.

Meeting after ʿAṣr

I was scheduled for a long meeting with our group after ʿAṣr in which I answered various questions on marriage, selecting spouses, regulations of travel, required covering for females, female dress and rules of gender interaction.

We went to Ṣalāḥ al-Dīn Street to buy dates and some gifts, and returned shortly before sunset time to break our fast at the hotel.

ʿIshāʾ Prayer

We prayed ʿIshāʾ and Tarawīḥ prayers at al-Aqṣā Mosque, and the Imām prolonged his supplication in the Witr prayers calling for the liberation of al-Aqṣā Mosque.

Sermon on the Mount of Olives

Zayd had scheduled a meeting for us on the Mount of Olives. There I engaged in a commentary on Sūrah al-Tīn, inspired by the views of Ḥamīd al-Dīn Farāhī (d. 1349/1930).[113] I will summarize here what relates to the Mount of Olives, and those who want further details should examine his tafsīr.

> *CONSIDER the fig and the olive, (1) and Mount Sinai, (2) and this land secure! (3) Verily, We create man in the best conformation; (4) and thereafter We reduce him to the lowest of low (5) excepting only such as attain to faith and do good works: and theirs shall be a reward unending! (6) What, then, [O man,] could henceforth cause thee to give the lie to this moral law? (7) Is not God the most just of judges? (8)*[114]

The main point of the sūrah is to prove the notion of reward and establish the judgment of God, who is All-Just. It begins with an oath on four things, and the oath serves to prove the notion of certain reward through four worldly realities.

The fig and the olive referenced in the sūrah are two mountains, the first being in Iraq and the second this very mountain upon which we were standing. Mount Sinai is well known, and 'this land secure' is Makkah. These four regions are sites of historical judgement which proved that the Lord of mankind deals with them in mercy and justice according to their actions. The site of the fig represents the first manifestation of judgement upon mankind. It is the mountain of Jūdī referred in the Qur'ān:

> *And the word was spoken: "O earth, swallow up thy waters! And, O sky, cease [thy rain]!" And the waters sank into the earth, and the will [of God] was done, and the ark came to rest on Mount Jūdī. And the word was spoken: "Away with these evildoing folk!"*[115]

On the Mount of Olives the great judgment occurred where the religious trust and law was taken away from the Jews and given

---

[113] Great Indian scholar of the Qur'ān who inspired a generation of 20th century scholars.

[114] Qur'ān: Chapter 95.

[115] Qur'ān 11:44.

to another branch of the lineage of Ibrāhīm after what happened at the end of the reign of 'Īsā. He had spent a night on the Mount pleading to his Lord until dawn, having given up on his people and full of extreme sorrow over finding out that the Jews had resolved to kill him. Because of that, they were cursed and stripped of the trust which was instead given to a people more worthy of it. 'Īsā stated:

> Jesus said to them, "Have you never read in the Scriptures: 'The stone the builders rejected has become the cornerstone; the Lord has done this, and it is marvelous in our eyes'? Therefore I tell you that the kingdom of God will be taken away from you and given to a people who will produce its fruit. Anyone who falls on this stone will be broken to pieces; anyone on whom it falls will be crushed."[116]

This is the removal of the Kingdom of God which took place on the Mount of Olives, which is also summarized in the Gospel attributed to Luke:

> **Jesus Prays on the Mount of Olives**
>
> Jesus went out as usual to the Mount of Olives, and his disciples followed him. On reaching the place, he said to them, "Pray that you will not fall into temptation." He withdrew about a stone's throw beyond them, knelt down and prayed, "Father, if you are willing, take this cup from me; yet not my will, but yours be done." An angel from heaven appeared to him and strengthened him. And being in anguish, he prayed more earnestly, and his sweat was like drops of blood falling to the ground. When he rose from prayer and went back to the disciples, he found them asleep, exhausted from sorrow. "Why are you sleeping?" he asked them. "Get up and pray so that you will not fall into temptation."

[116] Matthew 21:42-4. New International Version.

Jesus Arrested

> While he was still speaking a crowd came up, and the man who was called Judas, one of the Twelve, was leading them. He approached Jesus to kiss him, but Jesus asked him, "Judas, are you betraying the Son of Man with a kiss?" When Jesus' followers saw what was going to happen, they said, "Lord, should we strike with our swords?" And one of them struck the servant of the high priest, cutting off his right ear. But Jesus answered, "No more of this!" And he touched the man's ear and healed him. Then Jesus said to the chief priests, the officers of the temple guard, and the elders, who had come for him, "Am I leading a rebellion, that you have come with swords and clubs?"[117]

It is mentioned in Sūrah al-Tīn that God deals with human beings with wisdom and establishes one nation after another who are given the trust. He raises some nations while lowering others in order to deal with them in accordance with how they fulfilled their trust. He says:

> *For, He it is who has made you inherit the earth, and has raised some of you by degrees above others, so that He might try you by means of what He has bestowed upon you. Verily, thy Sustainer is swift in retribution: yet, behold, He is indeed much-forgiving, a dispenser of grace.*[118]

Clashes

We returned to the hotel at 1:30 am and were surprised to see open clashes between Palestinians and the Israeli police on the streets close to the hotel. The police had closed entrances to the old town and barred the Palestinians from entering or exiting. They had placed iron barriers on the perimeter of the doors amid the increased tension which continued until the next day.

---

[117] Luke 22:39-52. New International Version.
[118] Qur'ān 6:165.

OVERLOOKING THE HOLY LAND

11

OVERLOOKING THE HOLY LAND

Wednesday 28th Ramadan 1436 AH

We prayed Fajr prayers confined to the hotel because of the unrest of the previous night. This issue had pre-occupied the minds of people. Everyone was speaking about it while having their pre-dawn meal.

Shopping

We left the hotel around 11:00 am for shopping. The ban was lifted and the traffic in the streets and roads had returned to normal. We walked around Ṣalāḥ al-Dīn Street without buying anything, pushed into narrow alleyways between the Ghawānimah and Qaṭṭānīn Gates. We walked through shops enjoying the sights, rubbing shoulders with buyers and sellers. We encountered individuals who were not worried like we were, and we felt alienated from their concerns. These ancient shops reminded me of a past that engendered deep emotions within myself, great love and affection for these people, full of delicious forbearance.

Library

I went to the library of the Al-Aqṣā Mosque to meet our brother Shaykh Yūsuf al-Uzbekī who happened to be late. After I enquired about him, a woman in charge of the women's studies department at the library called him and told me that he would come in the afternoon. I spoke to her for a while about our mutual interests. I then went with my family to Bāb Nāẓir and strolled around the shops and alleyways before praying Ẓuhr near Bāb al-Silsilah.

Shaykh Yūsuf Uzbekī

We then went to the library to see Shaykh Yūsuf only to find out that he was in a meeting. He would not come out to us until 2:00 pm. I went to the bookshelves and perused books until I came across a book of his. I began to study it and go through its contents. When the shaykh arrived, we spoke at length about Ijāzah, narrating ḥadīth, and researching books and manuscripts. He gifted me the catalogue of the books and manuscripts at the library, and we agreed to call him on the day of Eid so we could visit him in his village. I was pleased by the idea as I was keen to see more closely the lives of my brothers in Palestine in their own cities and villages.

Answering Questions

We went back to the hotel and took a little rest. I went down to the dining room around 3:00 pm for another question and answer session. I gave a brief speech and addressed questions about accommodation, travel, women's prayer and the difference of prayer between men and women.

Lesson on End of Ramadan

After supper, I gave a lesson close to the Rock on bidding farewell to the blessed month of Ramadan. The sign of accepted worship in Ramadan is that we spend our days and nights in anguish over the deprivation of its blessings along with even greater efforts to seek the Lord's pleasure through worshiping Him. This is because we do not worship Ramadan, but the Lord of Ramadan. The Qur'ān reminded us that when we lost our Prophet, peace be upon him, who was the source of all good, we were to continue to hold on to his way without compromising our submission to the Lord of the worlds:

> *Muhammad is no more than a Messenger, and Messengers have passed away before him. If, then, he were to die or be slain will you turn about on your heels? Whoever turns about on his heels*

> *can in no way harm Allah. As for the grateful ones, Allah will soon reward them.*[119]

When he passed, ʿUmar stood up to say, "By God, the Messenger of God has not died! God would raise him up and he would return to cut the hands and legs of people [who claimed he had died]." Abū Bakr came, uncovered the Prophet's face, and kissed his forehead, saying: "May my mother and father be ransomed for you, how beautiful you are in death as well as life!" He then left and addressed the people, "Whoever used to worship Muḥammad, then he has died. But whoever worships God, know that God is alive and will never die."

Those who worship Ramadhan should know that it has ended and moved on, and those who worship God should know that God is alive and will never die. He is ever-present and will never go away.

Mount Mukabbar

Then we went to Jabal al-Mukabbar, a mountain that overlooks most of Jerusalem's neighborhoods. It is reported that the second caliph ʿUmar b. al-Khaṭṭāb climbed it when he opened Jerusalem. Next to it there is a town called Jabal al-Mukabbar located to the southeast of Jerusalem. Most of its inhabitants are from the ʿUbaydī and Sawāḥira clans. The Romans built a church in the name of St. Parmesius on Mount Mukabbar while the British built an office for their high commissioner and established the Arab College.

Lesson on the Mount

I spoke on the mountain about the promise of God to the Muslims by making them inherit the land of Ibrāhīm and establish the faith that God chose for them, and about the conquest of Jerusalem during the caliphate of ʿUmar.

---

[119] Qurʾān 3:144.

When Abū 'Ubaydah b. al-Jarrāḥ completed the opening of Damascus, he besieged Jerusalem and petitioned the residents for peace. They refused, as some of their priests claimed that the one who would conquer the city would fit a particular description. Abū 'Ubaydah wrote a letter informing 'Umar of this. He consulted his senior companions, and 'Uthmān was of the view that 'Umar should not go there in spite of their demands, whereas 'Alī suggested that he go in order to boost the morale of the Muslims besieging the city. He preferred the opinion of 'Alī and set out for Jerusalem with his army, while leaving 'Alī in charge of Madīnah. 'Abbās went ahead of him. 'Umar wrote to the heads of the army battalions that they come out to meet him at al-Jābiyyah[120] on a specific day mentioned in the letter, while leaving others in charge of their tasks. The first ones to meet him were Yazīd b. Abū Sufyān and Abū 'Ubaydah, followed by Khālid on horseback, who kept riding until he entered the pool. 'Umar descended from his mule, removed his shoes and waded in the water along with his mule.

Abū 'Ubaydah said to him, "You have achieved something great among the people of the earth." 'Umar struck his chest and said to him, "If only someone other than you had said this, Oh Abū 'Ubaydah! You were the lowest and the least of people, hated by others, and God honored you with Islām. However much you seek honor elsewhere, God will only humiliate you."

'Umar then moved on and concluded a peace agreement with Christians of Jerusalem, conditioned on the withdrawal of the Byzantine troops. He entered the mosque from the same door that the Prophet, peace be upon him, had entered on the night of Isrā. It is said that he greeted Jerusalem when entering and prayed in the prayer niche of Dāwūd. He led the Muslims in Fajr the next morning, reciting sūrah Ṣād in the first rakah along with its extra prostration, and in the second rakah, sūrah Banī Isrā'īl. He then came to the Rock, guided to the location by Ka'b al-Aḥbār, who suggested that he construct a mosque behind it. 'Umar said to

[120] An important military camp of the Muslim armies in Syria.

him, "You still resemble the Jews," and instead situated the mosque in the direction of the qiblah, which is now the Qiblī, or 'Umarī Mosque. The opening of Jerusalem occurred in Rabīʿ al-Awwal in the year 16 AH.

After the lecture, there were many questions about working in restaurants where alcohol is sold, serving in non-Muslim armed forces, and others. One student asked, "The Companions would weep at reciting the Qur'ān but it doesn't move us. What should we be doing?" I replied with a lengthy answer that included the following, "The very worry of not being able to weep is considered weeping too."

EXPEDITION

12

EXPEDITION

Thursday 29th Ramadan 1436 AH

Expedition Competition

Zayd organized an expedition contest designed to hunt for the treasures the al-Aqṣā precincts. We all went to the mosque early enthusiastic about the idea and determined to win. We were divided into teams, with mine consisting of my family and a student named Sana. Each group was given a list containing 25 historical sites and monuments in al-Aqṣā Mosque, which we had to find. We were obliged to follow the designated order in the listing, which mixed random locations from all over al-Aqṣā—east to west, north to south, inside and outside the mosque—and made the contest all the more difficult.

The contest began at 10:15 am with every team serious about winning and spurring on one another every time they came across each other. An hour passed by and it got really warm on a day we were fasting. The effects of fatigue began to appear on our faces and the enthusiasm began to diminish, as some dropped out. Ultimately, only two teams were left in the competition: my own and one other. The competition between us was fierce while we were tired and exhausted. The competition finished at 3:00 pm with my team winning, praise God.

I then rushed to the hotel to deliver a scheduled lesson only to find out that it had been rearranged. I went up to my room instead to rest.

Sighting the Crescent of Shawwāl

The sighting of the crescent of Shawwāl was announced today and joy could be seen on peoples' faces. Masses began to gather in the streets in preparation for the day of Eid. Imām Yūsuf Abū Sneina honored us with a visit after dinner. We exchanged greetings, congratulations and even some gifts. I then delivered a speech about the passing of Ramadan, the reception of Eid, and an explanation of the Eid prayer according the Ḥanafī school.

Women's Meeting

I then had a session with women, in which I taught them the details of prayer with differences between individual and congregational forms, and between men and women.

EID ON FRIDAY

13

EID ON FRIDAY

Friday 1st Shawwāl 1436 AH

Combining Eid and Friday prayers on the Same Day

I prayed Fajr in the mosque, and while I was waiting for the Eid prayers some of my group members asked me of the case when Eid falls on a Friday. Do one of the prayers suffice for the other? I answered:

Jurists of the Ḥanafī school along with some others hold the view that both prayers must be independently fulfilled and do not suffice for the other. Other scholars opted for the concession of allowing one of the two prayers to be performed. Jurists have debated this issue at length. Probably the best summary of that is what Ibn Taymiyyah stated:

> When the Eid prayers and Friday prayers happen to fall on the same day, there are three scholarly views:
>
> 1. The Friday prayer is obligatory on the one who has performed the Eid prayer in the same way that it is obligatory every Friday, based upon the general evidences that prove its obligatory status.
> 2. The Friday prayer is not obligatory for those who live on the outskirts of the city, such as the slopes and valleys, because ʿUthmān allowed them to skip the Friday prayer after they had prayed Eid with him.
> 3. The last view, and the correct one, is that the ones who have performed Eid prayer do not have to perform the Friday prayer, but the Imam must conduct the prayer

for those who wish to attend and for those who have not prayed the Eid. This is what is reported from the Prophet, peace be upon him, and his Companions, like ʿUmar, ʿUthmān, Ibn Masʿūd, Ibn ʿAbbās, Ibn al-Zubayr and others. In fact, there is no reported difference on this from the Companions. Those early scholars who held a different view likely were not aware of the practice of the Prophet, peace be upon him, on the matter when Eid fell on a Friday. He prayed the Eid prayer and then allowed the concession of skipping the Friday prayer. In one report, he said after the Eid prayer, "Oh people, you have done well! Those who wish to attend the Jumuʿah should do so, for we will be gathering for it." Also, when a person attends the Eid prayer, the aim of community gathering is realized, and he can pray Ẓuhr in place of Jumuʿah. The Ẓuhr takes place within its time, while the Eid prayer fulfils the aim of Jumuʿah. Making Jumuʿah remain obligatory upon people would represent great hardship and also detract from the aim of Eid as well as the joy and celebration that is legislated therein. When one refrains from Jumuʿah then the Eid reverts to its original intent, because Jumuʿah is also an Eid (celebration), as is Eid al-Fiṭr and the Day of Sacrifice. The way of the Legislator is that when two similar acts of worship coincide, one of them merges into the other, as wuḍūʾ is a sub-part of ghusl (washing). And God knows best.[121]

Eid Prayer

The Imām led the Eid prayer. In the first rakʿah before al-Fātiḥah, he performed seven takbīrāt,[122] and in the second rakʿah, five, as it

[121] Pg. 364-5. Ibn Taymiyyah. *al-Fatāwā al-Kubrā*. Dār al-Kutub al-ʿIlmiyyah.
[122] See footnote 101.

was narrated from the Prophet, peace be upon him, that he said: "There are seven takbīrāt in the first rak'ah and five in the second, and recitation of the Qur'ān after both of them."[123] The scholars differed concerning the details of these takbīrāt, but this is not a place for this discussion.

The Imām delivered a two-part sermon after the prayer, with frequent takbīrāt throughout. In fact, this entire place has been buzzing with this practice of takbīrāt since the Fajr prayer at dawn. The Imām during the sermon called people to honor their parents and relatives, and then called their attention to the dire situation in Palestine, including the forced siege of Gaza and the numerous prisoners. He prayed for the release of the prisoners and the removal of oppression. I thought at this moment that if these supplications might even be answered by the Lord on behalf of non-Muslims praying for their loved ones, so how would He not respond to the believers who possess the faith of Islām, for He is Ever-Merciful towards them?

While leaving the prayers, I saw followers of various Islamic movements chanting slogans condemning the oppressors and renewing their resolve to take back their holy sites and the lands of Palestine from them.

Breakfast at the Hotel

We returned to the hotel and had breakfast in its restaurant while exchanging holiday greetings. I was asked about greetings, hugs and handshakes, as well as the practice of giving gifts. I replied in the best way I could.

Friday Prayer

We entered the mosque for Friday prayer at 12:45 pm and found it empty. People had taken the concession of only praying the Eid

[123] Abū Dāwūd: Kitāb al-ṣalāh—Bāb al-takbīr fī 'īdayn.

prayer today. We prayed in the middle of the Qiblī Mosque close to the position of the Imam.

Shaykh Abū Sneina gave the sermon in which he said:

You have lived through blessed days in the month of Ramadan and God accepts the worship of those who are pious and sincere. The sincere ones are those who work for God's sake alone. God facilitated for you to pray in this al-Aqṣā Mosque, so congratulations to you! God says, "*Say: the enjoyment of this world is little while the Hereafter is better for those who are fearful of God.*"[124]

The Imām then called people to repent and seek forgiveness, and to reduce their talking, sleeping and eating. He also said: "Beware of sinning. Fear God, and be patient, steadfast and firm. Increase in seeking God's forgiveness throughout the night and day."

He stood up for the second sermon and said: "Eid is not just about wearing new clothes." He then referenced the siege and made a series of supplications—may God answer them all, for He is ever Responsive and Near.

Lesson on the Will of Ibrāhīm and Yaʿqūb

We went to al-Aqṣā Mosque at 3pm for my scheduled lesson inside Qiblī Mosque concerning the will of Ibrāhīm and Yaʿqūb:

> *And Ibrāhīm also enjoined upon his children to follow the same way, and Yaʿqūb did the same. His last will was, "O my children, God has chosen the same way of life for you. Hence, remain in submission up to your last breath." Were you present at the time when Yaʿqūb was on the point of death? He asked his children, "Whom will you worship after me?" They all answered, "We will worship your God and the God of your forefathers Ibrāhīm, Ismāʿīl, and Isḥāq: one God alone, and to Him we will submit."*[125]

[124] Qur'ān 4:77.

[125] Qur'ān: 2:131-2.

I informed them here that the reference here is complete and total submission to God. This is the submission of the heart and limbs. When the limbs externally submit without the presence of the heart, then transgression, hypocrisy and corruption appear. We ask God for sincere faith, good conduct, and accepted deeds, all in complete devotion and submission.

Visit to Jaffa

After ʿAṣr prayer, we rode a bus to the city of Jaffa passing by Bāb al-Lud and Bāb al-Ramlah. Jaffa is located on the coast of the sea and is about 55 km west of Jerusalem. It is a Canaanite name that means 'beautiful' or 'beautiful place.' It has one of the oldest harbors in the world, going back more than four thousand years. The Zionists seized the area and expelled the inhabitants in the infamous exodus of 1948.[126] Today, the local native Palestinian population, Muslim and Christian, is exceedingly small.

Coastal Restaurant

We had dinner at the coastal Abū al-ʿĀfiyah Restaurant overlooking the sea in Jaffa, renowned for its ethnic ambiance, authenticity, and adherence to traditional norms of Arab hospitality. It attracts customers and tourists from all over the country and the world. Perhaps the most notable dish is the seafood which is prepared and served in an ancient manner which includes a traditional oven. It is a large and upscale restaurant always filled with customers. Unfortunately, it pained us to witness men and women celebrating Eid by wearing clothes far removed from the norms of modesty and exhibiting behavior that could be considered immoral and licentious. We left the place as quickly as we could and prayed Maghrib in a large nearby mosque.

[126] Usually referred to as the Nakbah, or "catastrophe."

Tel Aviv

We boarded a bus which took us to an old Turkish mosque near Tel Aviv called the Ḥasan Bek, or Ḥasan Bey Mosque. It towers on the coast over the Mediterranean Sea on the highway to Jaffa and is considered one of the most famous historical mosques in the region. It is characterized by unique Ottoman architectural styles and was named after Ḥasan Bek, the Arab ruler of the town of Jaffa during Ottoman rule.

We walked around the coast for close to an hour, enjoying the pleasant breeze and beautiful sight. We came across a tavern that was burnt, it is said, by a suicide bomber and subsequently closed.

We saw Palestinian families enjoying Eid on the coast, and once again, we were dismayed by the immodest clothing. Where are the scholars and preachers, whose job is to remind and teach?

Our Return to Jerusalem

We boarded the bus at 10:00 pm and on the way back, I was asked about Sufism, spiritual pledges, Sufi orders, fasting six days of Shawwāl, combining obligatory with optional fasts and the status of Islamic institutions in Britain.

They also asked me about Shaykh Abū al-Ḥasan ʿAlī Nadwi and my connection with him, so I shared a brief biography. They asked me about the Islamic belief in destiny, and who were the best writers in Urdu. In response, I mentioned the names of Shiblī al-Nuʿmānī, Sayyid Sulaymān Nadwī, Maulānā Abū al-Kalām Āzād, and Maulānā Abū al-Aʿlā Mawdūdī.

We arrived at the hotel after 11:00 pm and I called Shaykh Yūsuf Uzbekī. We mutually agreed to visit his village tomorrow afternoon. The women in our group had cooked food for Eid and complained that I did not eat with them, so I obliged and had tea with them. We spoke about the history of al-Aqṣā Mosque, the Temple of Solomon, and Herod's Temple.

EXPLORING OUTSIDE JERUSALEM

14

EXPLORING OUTSIDE JERUSALEM

Saturday 2nd Shawwāl 1436 AH

Al-Eizariya Village

I set out with my family at 11:00 am via taxi to the al-Eizariya village.[127] We drove through winding roads between mountains and valleys, surrounded by lush vegetation that stood in direct view of the Sacred House whose surroundings God had blessed. Our bodies were stuck in this place and time, while our spirits traveled towards the pure souls God had created to live in, or travel through, this blessed place.

We arrived at the village in a half hour which seemed as if we had crossed thousands of years. It was as if Miʿrāj was a sustenance that is portioned out to anyone who has deep love for the land of Isrā and Miʿrāj.

Al-Eizariya is located at the foot of the Mount of Olives 2 km east of Jerusalem. It is bordered to the south by the town of Abu Dis, and to the west by Ras al-Amud and al-Aqṣā Mosque. Its sites include the mosque of the prophet Uzair, an ancient monastery, arches, the tomb of Lazarus, and an ancient hotel that was built on the road to Jericho by Umayyad ruler ʿAbd al-Mālik Marwān to accommodate travelers to al-Aqṣā.

This village is surrounded by colonies of Jewish settlers. They are unnaturally cut off from the blessed land, cut off from God's

[127] Named after Lazarus, the town is also known by the medieval name Bethany.

worship and the traditions of great prophets and messengers, and engrossed in worldly love and desires coupled with arrogance.

Uzair Mosque

I did not have the address to the house of Shaykh Al-Uzbekī so we came to the Uzair Mosque in the village to wait for him. Considered the second oldest in Jerusalem after al-Aqṣā mosque, the mosque is still active with full prayer services. The following is written on the mosque: "The Uzair Mosque was founded in the time of Ṣalāḥ al-Dīn when he liberated Jerusalem in 583/1187. It was renovated in the era of Ẓāhir Baybars in 670/1271." It continued to undergo various renovations during the Ottoman period by the Sulṭān 'Abd al-Ḥamīd II in 1316/1899. He renovated it in stages and built a minaret in 1373/1953. Next to the mosque is a church which bears the inscription 'Tomb of the Prophet Uzair.'

The local worshipers welcomed us warmly. My family went to the special area for women while I contacted Shaykh Yūsuf. He welcomed us and informed us that he was on his way.

There was a place in the mosque which provides cold water where children come to drink frequently. My heart was pained to see them with hairstyles[128] imitating the Jews and listening to their music.

We soon met Yūsuf Uzbekī and walked with him as he recounted the history of the mosque and described some of its landmarks. He informed us that some people claim that this is the tomb of the prophet Uzair and that this is the village that he had visited when he famously asked, "How will God bring this to life after its death?"[129] Others claim that this was the village of Lazarus, one of the disciples of Jesus, whom he raised from the dead.

[128] The specific style referenced here is known as *qaza'* and was forbidden by the Prophet. It consists of shaving part of the head completely while leaving out other portions.

[129] Qur'ān 2:259.

Al-Quds University

Shaykh Uzbekī took us in his car to Abu Dis. We passed through the large security wall which is a barrier between its residents and Jerusalem. It is called the Apartheid Wall. The neighborhood is only a ten-minute walk from al-Aqṣā Mosque, and the Dome of the Rock is visible while the call to prayer is heard. However, the residents are forbidden from praying there. On a practical level, the wall has split the community and separated families from one another.

We walked around the university and combined Ẓuhr and ʿAṣr prayers in the university mosque. The university was founded in 1984 with its main building located in the city of Abu Dis amidst four campuses which include the Faculty of Literature, Science and Technology, Medicine and Pharmacy, Fiqh and Law, Qurʾān and Islamic Studies, Foundations of Religion, Education, Management and Economics.

Village of Abu Dis

We toured the village of Abu Dis, which is east of Jerusalem and adjacent to it. Its construction possibly dates back to the Roman era, and Ṣalāḥ al-Dīn later encamped here. It contains a mosque attributed to him.

Shaykh Ḥusām al-Dīn

In the village, we visited the great scholar Shaykh Ḥusām al-Dīn Mūsā ʿAffānah. He is a scholar, jurist, well-known author and professor of jurisprudence at al-Quds University. He is the director of a multi-volume work as well as television series entitled 'Yasʾalūnak' where people ask questions of jurisprudence. He was born in the town of Abu Dis 1374/1955 and graduated from the Islamic University of Madīnah and Umm al-Qurā University.

His writings include a PhD thesis on exploring new meanings in the realm of uṣūl al-fiqh, a multi-volume jurisprudential work entitled *Yas'alūnak*, a critical edition of Jalāl al-Dīn Maḥallī's commentary on *al-Waraqāt fī Uṣūl al-Fiqh*, multiple legal edicts, a work on the ḥadīth narrations pertaining to the saved sect, and many others.

He welcomed me in his home and spoke about his studies in Makkah and Madīnah. He asked me about my research interests and works in Arabic and English. He lavishly praised the scholars of India, especially Abū al-Ḥasanāt 'Abd al-Ḥayy of Lucknow. I introduced him to the great scholar Ḥamīd al-Dīn Farāhī and his Qur'ānic works and spoke about his work on Qur'ānic coherence.

He shed some light on the relationship between the great scholar and warrior Amīn Ḥusaynī and our teacher Shaykh Abū al-Ḥasan 'Alī Nadwi. He stressed that it was his intent to start a separate department and library in al-Quds University to specifically research al-Aqṣā Mosque. This project would cost about half a million dollars, and various Turkish organizations have pledged that amount already.

Finally, the Shaykh gifted some of his books to me.

Excessive Force

We returned by bus to the hotel at 3:45 pm. On the way, we passed through security checkpoints. Two soldiers jumped aboard our bus and pointed their rifles while speaking to the Palestinian passengers among us in a violent tone. They removed several passengers from the bus, which included my daughters Fāṭimah and 'Ā'ishah. My protests only made them angrier. They ejected my entire family and forced us to enter a long security line which was in a completely enclosed space like a vault. They searched us all extensively. I was quite dismayed by their excessive use of force and surprised at what the native population has to endure in terms of fear and terror.

Lod Gate

We left the hotel at about 6:00 pm to visit Lod Gate (Bāb al-Ludd). We passed through roads lined with gharqad[130] trees. This is a low-lying shrub with no trunk along with intricate, entangled branches and hard, poisonous thorns. It has an unpleasant smell, and its fruit is not edible. Its leaves are tiny and yellow-green in color. Ḥadīth narrations describe it as the trees of the Jews. The Prophet, peace be upon him, said:

> The Hour will not begin until Muslims fight the Jews, until a Jew will hide behind a rock or a tree, and the rock or tree will say: 'O Muslim, O slave of God, here is a Jew behind me; come and kill him'–except the gharqad tree for it is the tree of the Jews.[131]

At 6:30 pm, we arrived at Bāb al-Ludd, which is around two miles from Ramla. Here, I spoke to the group about the Dajjāl (anti-Christ) and related to them several ḥadīth narrations which reveal that ʿĪsā son of Maryam will descend at the white minaret to the east of Damascus. Then Dajjāl will appear and the believers will gather in the holy land. Dajjāl will flee and ʿĪsā will catch up with him at the eastern portion of Bāb al-Ludd and kill him. Also, Dajjāl upon seeing ʿĪsā will begin to dissolve like salt in water. Had he left him, he would have perished, but, ʿĪsā was destined to kill him at Lod Gate.

Indian Hospice

We returned to the hotel at about 7:30 pm and had dinner. We headed to the mosque for ʿIshāʾ prayer, and on the way, we visited the Indian Hospice (al-Zāwiyah al-Hindiyyah) close to Bāb al-Sāhirah. It was constructed to commemorate the visit of the famous Indian Sufi scholar Bābā Farīd al-Dīn Masʿūd Ganj Shakar (d. 664 AH), a senior scholar of the Chisti order.

130 Also known as boxwood, or boxthorn trees.
131 Ṣaḥīḥ Muslim: Kitāb al-fitan wa ashrāṭ al-sāʿah.

There is a large courtyard surrounded by trees, rooms, a kitchen, a mosque and a room attributed to Bābā Farīd. There is also a library and photo exhibition with historic as well as contemporary photos of prominent Palestinian and Indian figures who have visited the zāwiyah.

Shaykh Abū Sneina

After 'Ishā' prayers, we met Shaykh Yūsuf Abū Sneina and then went to Ṣalāḥ al-Dīn Street to shop, only to find the shops closed due to Eid. We returned to our hotel and found Shaykh Abū Sneina waiting there with some gifts. Then we ascended to the roof of the hotel, where I recorded a short video clip for Al-Buruj Press about my impressions of this trip.

BIDDING FAREWELL

15

BIDDING FAREWELL

Sunday 3rd Shawwāl 1436 AH

Shrine of Yūnus

We prayed Fajr at al-Aqṣā Mosque and had an early breakfast while the birds were still in their nests. We then visited the village of Halhul in the Hebron district. We found the streets deserted and could not see any passenger nor pedestrian. We had arrived at 6:30 am and visited the mosque of Yūnus, peace be upon him. It also contains a shrine attributed to him though there is no historical proof for this. It is claimed that an ancient mosque was built over his grave, and that the minaret was built by the Ayyūbid king ʿĪsā Sharaf al-Dīn, nephew of Ṣalāḥ al-Dīn, in 1226 CE. Only a small part of the ancient mosque and minaret remained, which became part of the modern Grand Mosque.

The mosque had separate prayer spaces for men and women. The men's hall was empty, while that of the women had a number of worshippers. We found an elderly woman weeping and making fervent supplications, and decided to ask her what was wrong. She told us that her son had been imprisoned without charge. She had no one to turn to but God. She asked us to pray for her predicament too.

The city of Halhul is located on the central Palestinian plateau in the West Bank, 5 km from Hebron and 30 km from Jerusalem. It is famous for farming and agriculture. It has a school dating back to the Ottoman period. It is said that the reason for its name is because the Prophet Yūnus, when he was spit out by the whale on the coast, had settled in the mountains of this town for an entire year until he healed, before setting out for his own land. In Arabic '*ḥalla ḥawl*', meaning 'he spent a year', became combined into Halhul. It is also said that the name means 'giant man,' implying that this was a 'land of giants.' It could also be that the name means a land where plants and vegetation are in abundance.

Shrine of Prophet Lūṭ

We then drove to the village of Banī Na'īm passing through the well of Shaba'. There, we visited the shrine of the Prophet Lūṭ (Lot). Inscribed over the shrine is the following: "In the name of God, Most Gracious, Most Merciful. This building of the shrine of the Prophet of God, Lūṭ, peace be upon him, was restored by Maulānā Sulṭān al-Malik al-Ẓāhir Barqūq, may God preserve his kingdom forever, and may the blessings of God be on Muḥammad, his family and companions."

Located 7 km east of Hebron, the village of Banī Na'īm is also part of the Hebron Governorate. It was known in the Roman era as the village of Caphar Barucha, and after the Arab Islamic conquest, as Kafr Barīk. The Arab clans of Banū Nu'aym settled there and gave it its current name. There are more than eighteen mosques in the city, the most important of which is the mosque attributed to the Prophet Lūṭ. There also exist remnants of an ancient high wall that was square shaped, with towers on each corner, likely dating to the Roman era.

Interpretation of the last ten chapters

We turned back to Jerusalem before high noon and headed to the Dome of the Rock, where I had a lecture on the last ten chapters of the Qur'ān. Zayd recorded the lecture for the benefit of students and those wishing to understand the meaning and message of the Qur'ān.

Return Home

We combined Ẓuhr and 'Aṣr prayers in al-Aqṣā Mosque and bade it a final farewell, while firmly resolving to return again, frequently, in good faith and in good health. We went back to the hotel to have lunch and pack our bags for the journey back home. Eventually, we arrived back in the United Kingdom safe and sound, praise be to God and peace and blessings upon our Prophet Muḥammad, his family, Companions and followers until the end of time.

REFERENCES

Abū Ghuddah, ʿAbd al-Fattāḥ. *Ṣafaḥāt min Ṣabr al-ʿUlamāʾ*. Aleppo, Syria: Maktabah Al-Maṭbūʿāt al-Islāmiyah. 1394/1974.

Al-ʿAsqalānī, Ibn Ḥajar. *Fatḥ al-bārī*. 2nd edition. Egypt: Dār al-ʿĀlamiyyah. 1436/2015.

Beg, Muḥammad al-Khuḍarī. *Itmām al-Wafāʾ fī Sīrat al-Khulafāʾ*. Beirut: al-Maktabah al-Thiqāfiyah. 1402/1982.

Ibn Kathīr, Abū al-Fidāʾ. *Al-Bidāyah wa al-Nihāyah*. Cairo: Dār al-Taqwā. 1420/1999.

Brown, Jonathan A.C. *Hadith: Muhammad's Legacy in the Medieval and Modern World*. London, UK: Oneworld Publications. 2nd edition. 2018.

Bukhārī, Muḥammad b. Ismāʿīl. *Ṣaḥīḥ al-Bukhārī*. Damascus: Dār al-Nawādir. 1433/2012.

Dhahabī, Shams al-Dīn Muḥammad b. Aḥmad. *Siyar aʿlām al-nubalāʾ*. Beirut, Lebanon: Muʾassasat al-Risālah. 11th edition. 1417/1996.

Dhahabī. *Tārīkh al-islām wa wafayāt al-mashāhīr wa al-aʿlām*. Beirut: Dār al-Kutub al-ʿIlmiyah. 1426/2005.

Al-Ghaṣn, ʿAbdullah b. Ṣāliḥ. *Daʿāwā al-Munāwiʾīn li Shaykh al-Islām Ibn Taymiyyah*. Dammām, Saudi Arabia: Dār Ibn al-Jawzī. 1424.

Al-Ḥalabī, ʿAlī. *Mausūʿah al-āḥādīth wa al-āthār al-daʿīfah wa al-mauḍūʿah*. Riyad: Maktabah al-Maʿārif. 1419/1999.

Al-Ḥamawī, Yāqūt. *Muʿjam al-Udabāʾ*. Beirut: Dār al-Gharb al-Islāmī. 1993.

Al-Ḥarīrī, al-Qāsim b. ʿAlī. *Maqāmāt al-Ḥarīrī.* Beirut, Lebanon: Dār Ṣādir. No date given.

Hughes, Thomas Patrick. *Dictionary of Islam.* New Delhi, India: Oriental Books Reprint Corporation. 1976.

Ibn ʿAsākir. *Tārīkh Madīnat Damishq*. Beirut: Dār al-Fikr. 1415/1995.

Ibn Khaldūn. *The Muqaddimah: An Introduction to History*. Translated by Franz Rosenthal. New Jersey, US: Princeton University Press. 2005.

Ibn Taymiyyah. *Majmūʿ al-fatāwā.* Madīnah, Saudi Arabia: Majmaʿ al-Mālik Fahd. 1425/2004.

Ibn Taymiyyah. *Majmūʿ al-fatāwā.* Manṣūrah, Egypt: Dār al-Wafāʾ. 3rd edition. 1426/2005.

Ibn Taymiyyah. *Tafsīr al-Kabīr.* Beirut: Dār al-Kutub al-ʿIlmiyah. 1433/2012.

Ibn Taymiyyah. *Iqtiḍāʾ al-Ṣirāṭ al-Mustaqīm li Mukhālafat Aṣḥāb al-Jaḥīm.* Riyadh: Maktabat al-Rushd. No date available.

Al-Jabartī, ʿAbd al-Raḥmān. *Ajāʾib al-Āthār fī Tarājim wa al-Akhbār.* Beirut: Dār al-Kutub al-ʿIlmiyah. No date given.

Kennedy, Hugh. *The Great Arab Conquests: How the Spread of Islām Changed the World We Live In.* Philadelphia: De Capo Press. 2007.

Muslim b. al-Ḥajjāj. *Ṣaḥīḥ Muslim.* Damascus: Dār al-Nawādir. 1433/2012.

Nadwī, Moḥammad Akram. *Man ʿAllamanī.* Lucknow, India: Dār al-Rashīd. 1440/2018.

Nadwī, Moḥammad Akram. *Shaykh Abū al-Ḥasan ʿAlī Nadwī: His Life and Works.* West Yorkshire, UK: Nadwi Foundation. 1434/2013.

Nadwī, Moḥammad Akram. *Lessons Learned: Treasures from Nadwah's Sages*, trans. Abu Zayd. New Jersey, USA: Quran Literacy Press. 2019.

Nadwī, Moḥammad Akram. *al-Dhikr al-Jamīl li Ayyām al-Quds wa al-Khalīl*. Beirut: Dār al-Bashā'ir al-Islāmiyah. 1439/2018.

Al-Shāfi'ī, Muḥammad b. Idrīs. *Dīwān al-Imām al-Shāfi'ī*. Homs, Syria: Maktabah al-Ma'rifah. 1392/1974.

Al-Shāri'ī, Muwaffaq al-Dīn. *Murshid al-Zuwwār ilā Qubūr al-Abrār*. Cairo: Dār al-Miṣriyah al-Lubnāniyah. 1415/1995.

Tamīm al-Marghūthī. *Fī al-Quds*. Cairo, Egypt: Dār al-Shurūq. 2009.

Al-Ṭā'ī, Abū Tamām. *Dīwān al-ḥamāsah*. Beirut, Lebanon: Dār al-Kutub al-'Ilmiyyah. 1418/1998.

INDEX

ʿAbd al-Fattāḥ Abū Ghuddah, 23, 58
ʿAbd al-Ḥamīd II, 46, 126
ʿAbd al-Majīd I, 51
ʿAbd al-Malik b. Marwān, 47, 48, 54, 78
ʿAbd al-Malik Marwān, 68
Abū al-ʿĀfiyah Restaurant, 122
Abū al-Ḥasan ʿAlī Nadwī, 136
Abū ʿAlī al-Q̲ālī, 98
Abū Sneina, xi, 17, 23, 55, 63, 66, 116, 121, 130
Abū Tamām, 1
Adhān, 9, 10, 19, 70, 81
Akram Ḍiyāʾ al-ʿUmarī, 23
Al-Eizariya, 125
Al-Q̲uds University, 92, 127, 128
Al-Zāwiyah al-Hindiyyah, 129
Ashrafiyyah School, 80
Bāb al-Asbāṭ, 15
Bāb al-Aswad (Lions Gate), 46
Bāb al-Ḥadīd (Iron Gate), 79
Bāb al-Ḥiṭṭah, 15, 18, 46, 86, 100
Bāb al-Jadīd, 46
Bāb al-Khalīl (Jaffa Gate), 46
Bāb al-Ludd (Lod Gate), 129
Bab al-Maṭharah (Ablution Gate), 79
Bāb al-Mazdūj (Double Gate), 46
Bāb al-Mufrad, 46
Bāb al-Nabī Dāwūd (Zion Gate), 46
Bāb al-Nāẓir, 78, 79, 86, 96, 104
Bāb al-Q̲aṭṭānīn, 79, 80, 101
Bab al-Q̲aṭṭānīn (Cotton Merchant Gate), 79
Bāb al-Raḥmah, 46, 53, 54
Bāb al-Sāhirah, 5, 46, 77, 129
Bāb al-Silsilah, 49, 64, 74, 80, 87, 88, 105
Bāb al-Tawbah, 53
Bāb al-Thulāthī (Triple Gate), 46
Bāb al-ʿUmūd (Damascan Gate), 46

Bāb Fayṣal, 15
Bāb Ḥiṭṭah, 64
Bāb Qaṭṭānīn Market, 103, 104
Bābā Ratan, 74
Banī Na'īm Village, 133
Baqīyy b. Makhlad, 89
Bethlehem, 40, 43
Bustān al-Muḥaddithīn, 22
Cemetery of Bāb al-Raḥmah, 54
Church of Saint Anne, 55
Church of the Holy Sepulchre, 50, 52
Church of the Nativity, 40
Dajjāl, 63, 129
Dār al-Gharb al-Islāmī, 23
Denis Michael Rohan, 87
Dome of Yūsuf, 81
Dr. Muḥammad Iqbāl, 12
Expedition contest, 115
Gatwick airport, 3
Gharqad tree, 129
Ghawānimah, 78, 100, 103, 108
Ghazālī Square, 54, 66, 68
Grammar Dome, 88
Halhul, 132
Ḥamīd al-Dīn Farāhī, 105, 128
Ḥanīfiyyah, 39, 82, 91
Harūn al-Rashīd Street, 5
Ḥasan Bek Mosque, 123
Hebron, 34-36, 39, 40, 88, 132
Ḥusām al-Dīn Mūsā 'Affānah, 96, 127
Ibn Khaldūn, 136
Ibn Taymiyyah, 33, 36, 118, 136
Ibrāhīm, 34-39, 82, 91, 106, 121
Ibrāhīmi Mosque, 35
Iḥyā' ' Ulūm al-Dīn, 54
Iḥyā' 'Ulūm al-Dīn, 61, 77, 82
Indian Hospice, 129
'Īsā Sharaf al-Dīn, 15, 132
Jaffa, 46, 122, 123
Journey of Abū Hatim al-Rāzī, 96
Khalīl b. Aḥmad al-Farāhīdī, 98
Khataniyyah Library, 48
Khiḍr, 59, 74
Kidron Valley, 29
King Faisal Gate, 47, 66, 78
Laylat al-Qadr, 11
Mahdī, 63
Maulānā Abū al-Ala Mawdūdī, 123
Mauristan, 52
Moroccan Gate, 46, 49, 87
Mosque of 'Umar, 43, 50
Mount Moriah, 16

Mount of Olives, 11, 29, 30, 63, 104-106, 125
Mount of Ṭūr, 29
Mountain of Jūdī, 105
Muḥammad ʿAlī Jawhar, 80
Muḥammad Amīn al-Shanqīṭī, 24
Muḥammad Ghazālī, 24
Muḥammad Ilyās Kāndehlawī, 21
Muḥammad Mutawallī Shaʿrāwī, 24
Mukabbar, 56, 111
Muqbil b. Hādī al-Wādiʿī, 24
Museum of Islamic Antiquities, 87, 94
Muṣṭafā al-Aʿẓamī, 23
Nāṣir al-Dīn al-Albānī, 24
Nebuchadnezzar II, 47
Prophet Ibrāhīm, 11
Prophet ʿĪsā, 29, 39-43, 63, 106, 129
Qādisiyyah School, 77
Qiblī Mosque, 16, 19, 20, 23, 61, 81, 92, 121
Qunūt supplication, 101
Rābiʿah al-ʿAdawiyah, 30, 31
Saʿīd b. al-Musayyab, 68, 69
Saʿīd Ḥawā, 24
Salāḥ al-Dīn, 19
Ṣalāḥ al-Dīn, 29, 31, 52-54, 56, 126
Salāḥ al-Dīn Street, 19, 104, 109, 130
Ṣalāḥī Hospital, 52
Ṣalāḥīyyah School, 55
Salmān al-Fārisī, 31
Sayyid Sulaymān Nadwī, 123
Shaykh Abū al-Ḥasan ʿAlī Nadwī, 21
Shaykh ʿAlī ʿAbbāsī, 21
Shaykh ʿIkrimah ʿAbdullah Ṣabrī, 70
Shaykh Mikkī Mosque, 77
Shiblī al-Nuʿmānī, 123
Shrine of the Shepherd, 32
Siyar aʿlām al-nubalāʾ, 30
Sulaymān b. ʿAbd al-Malik, 78
Sulaymān the Magnificent, 13, 29, 46, 95
Sulṭān Barsbay, 79, 95
Sulṭān Maḥmūd II, 78
Sulṭān Qaitbay, 80
Sūrah al-Tīn, 11, 104, 107
Tablīghī Jamāʿah, 21
Ṭālūt, 66
Tamīm Barghūthī, 14
Tankaz, 79, 88, 104
Tankazī School, 49, 88
Tel Aviv Airport, 4
Temple of Solomon, 49, 123

Tomb of Mūsā, 31, 32
'Omar al-Kiswānī, 92
Uzair Mosque, 126
Village of Abu Dis, 127
Wailing Wall, 49
Yūsuf al-Uzbekī, 96, 109
Yūsuf Uzbekī, 123, 126
Ẓāhir Baybars, 31, 126
Zāwiyah of Imām Ghazālī,
54

www.ingramcontent.com/pod-product-compliance
Lightning Source LLC
Chambersburg PA
CBHW041307110526
44590CB00028B/4279
9781915851024